Vesey Street

Children's Discovery Center

New York State Finance

Police

Chase

Citibank

5 WTC

Airline and Courier Services

Borders Books and Music

PA Police

HSBC Bank USA

Starbucks

Krispy Kreme

Church Street

J. Tobin Plaza

Gemelli

Gemelli Bar

Available

TKTS

4 WTC

Available

Available

Ferrara

Liberty Street

FROM THE INSIDE OUT

From the Inside Out

Harrowing Escapes from the Twin Towers
of the World Trade Center

September 11, 2001

Erik O. Ronningen

WELCOME RAIN PUBLISHING

NEW YORK

© 2013 by Ronningen Books, llc
New York

Published by Welcome Rain Publishers
230 Fifth Avenue
New York, NY 10001

Distributed in the United States by National Book Network

Photo © Jim Usher

ISBN 978-1-56649-384-0

Printed in the United States of America

Second Printing

Dedicated To

First Responders who performed their duty and paid the highest price—
Each of whom, trapped by circumstances, met his or her destiny;
Surviving families adjusting to their new normality;
All who made it out;
Those who kept me sane and balanced throughout the difficult years;
And all of my absent friends and colleagues, especially Douglas G.
Karpiloff & Sarah K. Ronningen.

With Love and Gratitude

Contents

PREFACE   IX

CHRONOLOGY OF EVENTS   XIII

I. WAKE-UP ALARM   5

II. ARRIVAL   II

III. IMPACT   29

IV. EVACUATION & ESCAPE   47

V. COLLAPSE   99

EPILOGUES   137

ACKNOWLEDGMENTS   153

MAP OF LOWER MANHATTAN, CIRCA 9/11/2001   154

PREFACE

IT WAS LATE THE EVENING OF SEPTEMBER 12, 2001. MY WIFE, SARAH, and I were discussing my near demise and the events of the prior morning, when out of the blue I had a foreign thought: write a book. I am not a writer save what one must put on paper in business, and the occasional correspondence to far-flung family and friends. But write a book is the thought that was given me.

I was just another one of the tens of thousands who awakened that beautiful Tuesday morning of September 11 and did what we all do—go to our places of business. But as we, and the world, were soon to learn it was no ordinary day—it was a painfully graphic example of how fragile our relationships are, and how we too often take them for granted. It was a wake-up call of many dimensions, and we learned that our lives can change in the time it takes the second hand of our watches to tick from one increment to the next.

I, too, like so many other thousands, was at my desk, high in the North Tower, minding my own business and preparing for a meeting when, in an instant, all our lives were changed forever.

In the months that followed, those of us who were the direct recipients of that fateful morning could talk only of where we were and how we escaped those quarter-mile-high structures. We focused entirely on the events surrounding that hour and forty-two minutes of our lives.

During this time I worked side-by-side with hundreds of Port Authority of New York and New Jersey employees who were coping—some better than others—with the effects of 9/11. And I heard some incredible stories: tales of near escapes, entrapments in free-falling elevators, fireballs storming through the lobbies, people trapped in the mall under the plaza or in stairwells when the towers collapsed, and others incarcerated by that incredible cloud of debris. People recounted breaking into automobiles and stealing boats, or being caught up in the animal instinct of stampeding panic. I heard remarkable stories of why people were, or were not, at their desks . . . everything from mental urges to get a doughnut, missed trains, forgotten pagers, and wrong coffee orders, to last-minute unscheduled meetings high in the tower, early subway exits to enjoy the beautiful day, and even secret trysts. I heard stories of people's courage, compassion, and selfless assistance to others though they put their own lives in harm's way. I heard people recount that God's angels led them from the pitch black of the collapse to the safety of the outdoors. I spoke with individuals who took months to return to work, and others who were still wrestling with survivor's guilt and feelings of responsibility for colleagues less fortunate than they. And I heard the stories that did not make the public press: the theft, greed, and cowardice of those who were less than "heroic," upstanding citizens.

I heard *hundreds* of personal experiences, each one as fascinating and harrowing as the one previous. Eventually I purchased a recorder, and I selected a couple dozen Port Authority employees—all with stories of terrifying and fascinating escapes—who agreed to discuss their experiences on tape and have their narratives published in a book. Those interviews were full of emotion: tears, sobbing, regrets of lost colleagues, and the occasional humor at the recollection of some comic episode. From normal people living their normal, everyday lives, I was gathering a valuable collection of the human experience—documenting that intangible essence of bravery, selflessness, and generosity of spirit that exists, often dormant, inside us all, rising to the forefront in times of crisis.

And though she was not in the towers, I included the experiences of my wife, Sarah, as a sampling of what our wives, husbands, children, and loved ones went through watching the events unfold on television: the horror of contemplating living out their lives without their noble companions.

At the end of about six months, everyone stopped talking. I suppose we were sick of hearing our voices telling the same stories over and over again. We focused on our businesses, began adjusting to the new "normal," and moved on with our lives.

My youngest sister, Kaia Rayburn, kindly volunteered to transcribe the thirty-plus hours of taped interviews, and presented me with stacks of copy and the digital transcriptions. It was my initial intent to publish in time for the first anniversary of 9/11. Then the fifth. But additional personal events began to interfere in my once-normal life, and I shelved a three-quarter-completed project.

Then I began to doubt the interest in 9/11. However, due to work responsibilities the first half-dozen years, I was frequently at the World Trade Center site and I would take time to walk the inside perimeter of the visitor's fence. There were thousands upon thousands of people from all over the U.S. and the world—countries I had never heard of, nor could pronounce—who had made the effort to navigate their way to southern Manhattan. I would spend an hour or two at a time answering their questions, giving them a little something extra to take home for their efforts to visit the site of our recently destroyed home.

I have been invited to speak to groups and gatherings on the anniversaries of 9/11. And on the eighth anniversary I had the privilege of speaking at the Lebanon Valley Chamber of Commerce's Annual Patriot Day Concert in Lebanon, Pennsylvania. There were fifteen hundred attendees in the audience. The event was standing room only, and I received an emotional standing ovation after speaking extemporaneously for forty minutes. These experiences made me realize how much people were still affected by 9/11, and that maybe a book was worth pursuing after all.

These past couple of years, thanks to the kind, gentle encouragement of many friends and colleagues, I seriously began to readdress my lack of interest, confronted the reluctance in my mind, and dusted off the old, incomplete manuscript.

The contents of this poor effort relate the experiences of more than a dozen "escapees" from high in the towers to the sub-basements and elsewhere in between. I hope I have been able to convey a little of what we all experienced that most remarkable, certainly unforgettable, and completely exhausting morning in our efforts to get from the inside out.

In fancy, put yourself in each of our places as you read these experiences; watch the American Airlines 767 fly into *your* office, feel the towers bend and twist, and hear the deafening explosions. Smell the smoke and aviation gas and be weightless in plunging elevators. Struggle for a breath of oxygen in acrid, smoke-filled stairwells. Run for your life as the fireballs chase you through the lobby. Hear the sickening sound of the poor unfortunates jumping to "safety." Experience the stampeding panic, and become engulfed in that evil black cloud. And, for a few moments you will be one of us: the privileged that made it out of the Twin Towers of the World Trade Center.

Over the course of the past ten-plus years, one individual asked that her contribution be pulled, and two others requested that their personal details be disguised. The experiences related are as accurate and dispassionate as I was able to craft them. Many reviewed their draft manuscript; others said to go with what I wrote. Any inaccuracies, embellishments, and errors of omission are mine alone, and I apologize to any who take umbrage with my license. And I thank all with whom I have had the privilege to be associated before, during, and after the life-changing events of that most memorable day.

Erik O. Ronningen
Mamaroneck, NY

CHRONOLOGY OF EVENTS

September 11, 2001

8:46 A.M. American Airlines Flight 11 from Boston, MA, to Los Angeles, CA, flies into the north face—floors 93 to 99—of the North Tower, Tower One of the World Trade Center

9:03 A.M. United Airlines Flight 175 from Boston, MA, to Los Angeles, CA, flies into the south face—floors 77 to 85—of the South Tower, Tower Two of the World Trade Center

9:59 A.M. Tower Two Collapses
The South Tower of the World Trade Center

10:28 A.M. Tower One Collapses
The North Tower of the World Trade Center

Note
Times are those established by the National Institute of Standards and Technology (NIST)

FROM THE INSIDE OUT

September 11
2:45 A.M.

THE TOWER SNAPPED SOMEWHERE DEEP DOWN IN THE BOWELS OF THE structure. The sound was like a bullwhip followed by distant, late summer thunder. The experience was unreal, dream-like, in slow motion. Through the grinding, twisting, echoing rumble, the quarter-mile-high structure slowly began to topple due east, like an extension ladder. I turned, and through the haze saw a woman standing not three feet from me. I grabbed her hand, and with all the authority I could muster, shouted, "Let's go to the high side and ride it down." We began running, one agonizing step after another . . . like running through knee-high mud. We struggled with excruciating slowness to the west side of the office, climbing, climbing, climbing because the floor kept getting steeper and steeper as the tower fell farther and farther east. Books, binders, and small articles began flying through the air, attacking us like mad hornets; then equipment tumbled across the floor. Desks and furniture began plummeting end-over-end, and it was impossible to avoid getting hit. "Keep climbing!" I yelled in slow motion. The sweat dripped off my forehead as I desperately dragged her along, "We gotta keep—"

"Wake up, Erik. Wake up!" my wife, Sarah, shouted, urgency and concern in her voice as she tried to shake me awake. "You're having a nightmare. What is it? What were you dreaming?" she asked, always a little shaken by the moaning and thrashing that took place whenever I had a dream, a nightmare, of this nature.

"It's okay," I mumbled, wiping the beads of sweat off my face. "Go back to sleep. I just had another dream of the tower toppling over. Everything's all right," I muttered, falling back into a fitful sleep.

I

WAKE-UP ALARM

4:30 A.M.

Edward Bonny and his wife, Pat, had taken Monday off. Both had experienced premonitions the evening before. It was as if some cloud were hanging over their heads—some tremendous cloud—and they both had taken it as a warning not to go to the World Trade Center that day. They heeded the warning.

On Monday evening, they each once again had the same premonition. Ed usually followed his first instincts. He acknowledged that they shouldn't go to the World Trade Center on Tuesday also, but began to rationalize the premonition . . . and he knew it was a mistake.

Ed had retired from the Port Authority of New York and New Jersey many years ago and was now employed as a consultant. As such, Ed got paid only when he presented himself for work, and on Tuesday, Pat, a Port Authority employee, had a training class in the North Tower.

Ed took their destiny into his own hands—they had, after all, taken Monday off without consequence—and made the decision to overrule Divine Inspiration. When his 4:30 a.m. alarm went off on Tuesday, September 11, it was business as usual.

It was time for Nancy Seliga to get up.

A Port Authority employee since she graduated from high school at age seventeen, Nancy was the building manager for the North Tower, One World Trade Center. While she loved her job, rolling out of bed was a little more difficult than normal this morning because she and her husband, Chuck, had just the day before returned from a long overdue and well-deserved four-day weekend of rest and relaxation in Delaware. It was also Chuck's birthday this Friday, and Nancy was planning a party. However, despite these distractions, Nancy was looking forward to getting back to work.

Driving the nine miles from her home to the New Jersey Transit train station, Nancy couldn't help but notice what a clear and beautiful day was dawning. *It's going to be a good day*, she thought, getting back into the groove of a familiar routine.

5:00 A.M.

Jerrold M. Dinkels considered himself a modest man—an average suburban guy, born and raised in Brooklyn, New York. Married twenty-eight years to his beautiful wife, Mary Ellen, they had three children: Marissa, about to turn twenty-three, was a nurse; Alex, age twenty-four, was in finance; and Michael, age twenty-five, was in medical school.

Jerry was employed by the Port Authority as an engineering program manager. Today, like every other day, he followed his normal routine. He awoke to his alarm at 5:00 a.m., kissed Mary Ellen good-bye, and went to the gym at 5:30 for an hour's workout and a shower, before taking the 7:00 a.m. LIRR—Long Island Rail Road—from his home in Oceanside, New York, to Penn Station, New York City. It was a normal day, with the exception of the clarity—spectacular! "On a clear day, you can see forever," he hummed, thinking of that old Alan Jay Lerner favorite.

5:30 A.M.

"The time is 5:30 a.m., Tuesday morning, and it is going to be a clear and beautiful day in New York City," the radio announcer broadcast to eighteen million inhabitants in the greater metropolitan area.

"Rise and shine, Erik," Sarah murmured cheerfully to her husband, Erik Ronningen, as he flung his right arm out to turn off the clock radio. "Don't forget," she reminded him, "You've got your meeting with Doug Karpiloff today." She was referring to a 9:00 a.m. meeting that would change Erik's job status from a temporary, long-term consultant with the Port Authority of New York and New Jersey to a position as a full-time employee . . . with all the benefits.

Erik completed his morning ablutions, and dressed in a dark-blue pin-stripe suit, white shirt, striped red tie, and new black Florsheim wing-tip shoes. He arrived at the Mamaroneck train platform in Westchester, New York, to await the 6:24 a.m. Metro-North train to New York City's Grand Central Terminal.

"Good morning, Walter," he offered, and the greeting was returned in kind. After six months of standing not two feet from each other, Erik had introduced himself to Walter Krownowski. It became a fast friendship, like reuniting with a close school chum after decades of separation.

Walter and Erik conversed on the trip to Grand Central Terminal, and both walked to the Grand Central subway station, getting on the IRT number-four express train to Brooklyn. As the express approached Walter's Fourteenth Street stop, Walter mentioned to Erik that there should be plenty of tourists visiting the World Trade Center's observation deck that day.

"With today's conditions and clear visibility," Erik replied, "the observation deck will be packed."

Shaking hands, Walter said, "Have a good day, Erik."

"And you too, Walter. See you tomorrow."

A couple of stops later, Erik got off at Fulton Street and exited the subway system into bright, beautiful daylight. The Twin Towers of the World Trade Center were brilliantly silhouetted by an azure-blue New Jersey sky. The day reminded him of his youth, working summers at the Leesburg, Virginia, airport, and he thought to himself, *a great day for flying . . .*

6:00 A.M.

Having punched the snooze button on the clock radio one too many times, Sonia Henriquez was running a little late—having just returned from a fabulous Caribbean vacation. She jumped out of bed, washed, put on her beige suit, drank a quick cup of coffee, and ran for the bus.

Sonia worked for the Port Authority on the sixty-eighth floor in Tower One. She wasn't required to be at her desk until nine, but preferred to be there no later than 8:45. Conscientious, she liked to get in a little early to organize her day. Sonia sighed; the day had just begun and already she was off her routine. Taking a deep breath, she tried to envision the soothing beaches of the Caribbean—peaceful memories that were fading all too quickly . . .

II

ARRIVAL

6:00 A.M.

A Port Authority police officer for twenty-one years, Officer David Lim, a member of the K-9 Unit, Explosive Detector Team, since 1997, was assigned to the World Trade Center Police Command. His friend and trusted partner, Sirius, a Golden Labrador Retriever, was responsible for sniffing out explosives, checking unattended packages, clearing VIP areas before important events, and patrolling the truck docks and investigating the cargo coming into the vast underground complex of the World Trade Center. A Ryder rental truck full of explosives had caused significant property damage, injured thousands, and killed six people in the bombing of February 26, 1993. Officer Lim and his explosive-sniffing partner were duty bound to prevent another terrorist bombing.

David loved his job. He was a first-generation Chinese American, and ever since he was a young lad helping his parents in their Chinese restaurant in Chinatown, he was in awe of the New York City policemen that came in to eat. They treated young David with respect, and he admired their uniforms, guns, and sense of calm authority in the way they helped people. David was inspired by these "men of the law," and knew from an early age that he was going to be a policeman.

Officer Lim had savored his commute from his home in Lynbrook, New York, to the World Trade Center this morning. He regretted knowing that he would miss most of such a beautiful day performing his daily duties inside the buildings. His partner, Sirius, was with him and he, too, seemed to appreciate the quality of the day, as he was particularly frisky this morning.

The daily change-of-shift roll call completed, David finished the hundred-and-one little details that went with being an officer of one of the finest police forces in the country. Snapping the leash onto Sirius's collar and releasing him from the "stay" command, David and Sirius performed their post–roll call duties, making their normal rounds of the numerous entrances of the World Trade Center, ending in the mall.

###

6:30 A.M.

It had been nearly three hours since Victor M. Guarnera had awakened to his 3:40 a.m. alarm, dressed, kissed his sleeping wife, Carmela, good-bye, and walked to the Metuchen, New Jersey Transit, train station under bright, sparkling stars. In the east there had been the first hint of what promised to be a beautiful sunrise, and Vic, a recreational private pilot and active member of the Civil Air Patrol, thought it would be a beautiful day for flying.

He exited the World Trade Center PATH station deep beneath the towers and walked to the basement parking office on the B-2 level, the second of six basement levels. This was Vic's first stop on his daily routine, and he wanted to get an update from Kenny Grouzalis on the truck dock operation. Vic was the chief technical advisor and manager for security systems for the World Trade Department, the Port Authority department that ran the day-to-day operations of the World Trade Center complex.

Completing his rounds at the visitor desks, Vic went up to his office on the thirty-fifth floor of Tower Two, the South Tower, to strap on his radio, make his daily report to Doug Karpiloff, director of security and life safety, and take care of a few daily chores.

###

6:50 A.M.

Nancy Seliga, always the first to arrive in the morning, unlocked the door to the office space on the twenty-first floor of Tower One. Six weeks prior, after a two-year bid process, Larry Silverstein Properties had signed a coveted ninety-nine-year lease on the World Trade Center complex. Nancy and the senior executives of the World Trade Department had had beautiful offices on the eighty-eighth floor, with glorious views overlooking New York Harbor, the Hudson River, and, on the north side of the tower, the magnificence that was Manhattan Island. During the past couple of weeks, the Silverstein Properties operations staff had displaced several World Trade Department executives, occupying their eighty-eighth-floor offices. The move from eighty-eight to twenty-one had been a disappointment to her and her coworkers, and Nancy was still trying to get over the change.

Her pager hadn't summoned her the past four days she had been away, so life was good as she sat at her desk going through paperwork, catching up, and preparing for her weekly staff meeting at 8:30 a.m.

7:00 A.M.

Forty-five minutes after a lopsided good-bye kiss and a mumbled "See ya tonight, sweetie . . . have a good day," Sarah Ronningen, Erik's wife of thirty-four years, got up to get ready for her job at the Greenwich Association of Realtors in Greenwich, Connecticut. She noticed what a remarkably beautiful day it was as she threw seeds out to the morning flock of birds patiently awaiting their daily ration.

One thing kept gnawing at the back of her mind that she couldn't quite shrug off: Erik's nightmare of the collapsing towers.

7:10 A.M.

"Good morning, Bay," Erik Ronningen said in greeting, initiating the normal daily banter with the folks at Fine and Shippero, an enormously popular deli in the mall of the World Trade Center.

"Large coffee with just a little milk, Erik?" Bay responded, teasing, handing him the already bagged extra-large cup with his left hand while illustrating "a little" by showing about a quarter inch of air between his right thumb and forefinger. By Erik's third consecutive day of ordering coffee to go over the past three years, Bay and Sam had already memorized his morning coffee preference, along with those of hundreds of other regulars.

"Just a little milk," Erik confirmed, chuckling at their little routine. Bay and Sam tended to have a heavy hand with the milk, and Erik joked that they were prone to giving him a large cup of coffee-flavored milk.

"Throw in a buttered roll this morning, would you please, Bay? Butter both slices," he added as an afterthought.

The block-and-a-half walk through the mall was uneventful. He nodded greetings to the regulars, and watched John Abruzzo, another Port Authority early arrival, expertly navigate his electric wheelchair through the growing crowds on the way to his sixty-ninth-floor office in Tower One.

"Good morning, Captain Whitaker. Good morning, Officer Lim," Erik greeted, ruffling and patting Officer Lim's partner, Sirius, as he passed the Banana Republic, approaching the revolving doors leading into the lobby of Tower One.

Erik's double-elevator trip, transferring at the forty-fourth-floor sky lobby to the seventy-first floor of Tower One, was ordinary in all respects. Morning pleasantries passed between the normal early birds as he walked, balancing his coffee and buttered roll in one hand, briefcase in the other, to his cubicle on the southeast side of the North Tower.

After booting up his computer and taking a sip of coffee, Erik took advantage of the view before plunging into the day's work. It was a spectacular vision that morning looking out across New York Harbor. Lady Liberty saluted, her torch raised high; Ellis Island was a little to the west; and the tourist ferries were already plying their out-of-town fares back and forth. Looking farther south was the Verrazano-Narrows Bridge, and out beyond, Sandy Hook, New Jersey, looked close enough to touch. It was on days such as this when he would tease visitors that if they squinted and squiggled their eyes *just right*, they could see the tip of the Washington Monument, or looking out the east windows, the top of the Eiffel Tower. It almost always worked . . . for a second.

The floor-to-ceiling windows were only eighteen inches in width, designed to prevent the feeling of acrophobia when you stood too close, and reflected Architect Minoru Yamasaki's fear of heights. They were a thrill to look out, especially during the magnificent sunsets.

7:45 A.M.

Captain Anthony R. Whitaker, "Tony" to his friends, a thirty-year veteran of the Port Authority Police Department, was captain of the World

Trade Center Police Command. Captain Whitaker ran a tight command. Because his department was so much in the public eye—and he liked it that way—he required his officers to be impeccably turned out: uniforms cleaned and pressed, trousers dressed, highly polished shoes, properly trimmed haircuts, and though it was his officers' least favorite requirement, caps to be worn at all times. For many of the eighty thousand people who worked in the World Trade Center complex every day, the Port Authority Police Department was their only contact with local law enforcement. Tony's goal was to make the World Trade Center employees feel safe and secure. He wanted them to know that they were under the protective umbrella of the Port Authority World Trade Center Police Command.

The 6:00 a.m. roll call and other administrative duties out of the way, Captain Whitaker liked to greet people on their way to work each morning. "Community policing," he called it. It demonstrated good leadership, or as he preferred to think of it, *personal example is without superiority.*

Captain Whitaker's preferred show of presence, or his "image spot," was in the mall just outside of the Banana Republic—the northwest corner to be exact. This location provided maximum visibility to his "clients" going to either tower. The revolving doors going into the main lobby of Tower One were about fifty feet to his left, due west, and into the main lobby of Tower Two, about two hundred feet south through the mall corridor that stretched between the Chase and Citibank banking centers. This was his self-appointed post until 9:00 a.m.

It is remarkable, Tony thought to himself, *how many faces I recognize as people walk by me going to their places of business.* He guessed that he recognized the faces of about 80 percent of the employees, and though he wouldn't claim it, he also knew many by their first names, and greeted them as such when they walked by. You could tell a lot about people by observing their faces and body language as they walked by. "Taking the pulse of the people," he phrased it.

The pulse seemed a little slow this morning, he thought, as he removed his pager from his belt, checking the time. It was 0842 hundred hours, or 8:42 a.m. Tony was surprised at how light the foot traffic was at this time of the morning. Then he remembered, putting his pager back on his belt, that it was the second Tuesday in September—September 11—Election Day.

###

7:53 A.M.

Arriving after a normal commute from his uptown Manhattan apartment, Tad Hanc, a civil engineer with the Port Authority, settled himself in at his desk on the north windows of the eighty-sixth floor of Tower One. He spread out the *New York Times*, carefully positioning his cup of morning tea on the back right side of his desk to avoid accidentally spilling it, and began his normal, daily routine. Tad enjoyed this quiet time to himself before his coworkers arrived at nine, and took advantage of it to relax, get a feel for what was happening in the world, and plan the workday ahead of him.

###

7:55 A.M.

Having ignored the premonition to stay home, Ed Bonny was now content from a full breakfast in the World Trade Center mall with his wife, Pat. After delivering her safely to her training class on the sixty-first floor, Ed Bonny was comfortably seated at his desk on the seventy-first floor of the North Tower. He was located in the northeast quadrant near the east windows of the 40,000-square-foot floor, 3,560 square feet shy of one square acre. "Close enough for government work," was the worn-out joke.

Ed was catching up on his paperwork—faxing, completing documents for signature, and putting the finishing touches on a report he wanted to get out. He wished to accomplish all this before he and John Fisher, another consultant, went to the Teleport, a Port Authority property on Staten Island. They were scheduled for a 10:00 a.m. meeting on a security project.

"Ed, are you ready to go yet?" John asked impatiently.

"John, I'll be right with you," Ed replied. This was Ed's meeting, but John was one of those "A-type" personalities. John really knew his business and was a great asset, but sometimes Ed wondered where the line was drawn between competence and a passion for his work that someday might get him into hot water.

"Let's go, Ed," John pressed. "I'm ready to go."

"Don't worry about it, John," Ed countered. "As soon as I get this stuff out of the way, I'll be right with you." Ed and John's history in business went back many years. They were friends, though at times the uninitiated wouldn't see it that way. Theirs was one of those unique associations where each agreed to disagree with the other. But in spite of their bickering, Ed knew that they made a good team.

"Okay, John," Ed announced. "I'll be ready in three minutes. Why don't you go down to the sub-basement and check out a Port Authority car for our drive to Staten Island?"

"About time!" John said, relieved to be on the way. "Don't get lost. I'll be waiting for you down there."

John was highly respected by his peers. He had a ready smile, was quick to pick up the tab for coffee, and enjoyed a good joke. But if you were a contractor, you didn't want to be sitting across the table from him. John knew business contracts, and he made certain that every minute detail was in its exact place. It was this expertise that Ed wanted on his side of the table at this morning's meeting.

8:00 A.M.

Sarah Ronningen began her eight-mile, fifty-minute drive to work in Greenwich, Connecticut. As she pulled out of the driveway of her Mamaroneck, New York, home, she turned on the radio and alternately listened to the local news and an oldies station. Mumbling unspeakables to herself at the annoying stop-and-go traffic up I-95, and singing along with old favorites, at 8:50 a.m. she finally pulled into her building's garage, parked, and turned off the radio just as a "breaking news flash" began.

8:05 A.M.

After Vic Guarnera made his report to Doug Karpiloff, he met Jitendra Mavadia, the Security Command's systems administrator, on the 107th floor of Tower Two. There was to be a 10:00 a.m. test and sign-off by the observation deck manager on a half-dozen security doors that had been upgraded. Vic wanted to do a pre-test testing to be certain that there would be no surprises for the test at ten. Forty minutes later, Vic and Jitendra returned to their respective offices: Jitendra to the Security Command Center on the twenty-second floor of Tower One, the North Tower, and Vic to the thirty-fifth floor of Tower Two, the South Tower. Vic felt confident that the 10:00 a.m. test would go without a hitch. Progress was being made and it felt good.

8:07 A.M.

Yvonne R. Barker, an African American with finely chiseled features, born and bred in Brooklyn, New York, was a senior composition specialist with the Port Authority.

Yvonne took the bus from Brooklyn into lower Manhattan each morning, and this particular morning reminded her of April in Paris. She had recently returned from a Paris vacation with her boyfriend. The mother of a beautiful daughter, Larrica, and the grandmother of an even more beautiful granddaughter, Oien, age six, Yvonne was planning a September 23 birthday party for her daughter. Additionally, she had just received confirmation on the time-share and airline reservations to attend an early November wedding for the son of one of her best friends—on the beach in Saint Martin. All her friends, many of whom she'd not seen in many years, would be there. Yvonne was ready for the trip, and really excited.

"Good morning, Flory," Yvonne greeted cheerfully to her boss, Flory Danish, as she passed his corner cubicle going to her workstation. With her new arrival schedule, she and Flory were the only two people in the office at this time in the morning.

"Ummmm . . . smells good, Yvonne," Flory said in reply to her greeting.

On her way up to her eighty-sixth-floor office in Tower One, Yvonne had stopped in the mall and purchased a steaming hot cup of cappuccino. Settling in, careful not to drip any onto her papers, Yvonne took a luxurious sip and sat back to savor the flavor, and the stunning view out over the East River.

"Hello," Yvonne said into the telephone, answering it after the first ring. It was her sister-in-law, and after a brief conversation to discuss the upcoming trip to the islands, she hung up, had another sip of cappuccino, and took one last look at the beautiful view out her window before turning to her computer to do the work a senior composition specialist was paid to do.

8:10 A.M.

Jerry Dinkels's daily workout completed, he arrived refreshed and invigorated at his office in the northwest corner of the twenty-second floor of Tower One. His supervisor, Achille Niro, the program division manager, had been out of the office for a few days, and had put Jerry in charge. Achille had returned this morning and Jerry was preparing to brief him in his office on the seventy-second floor, before Jerry's regular 9:00 a.m. Tuesday meeting with his staff on eighty-two. Jerry was relieved that Achille had returned; now he could get back to focusing on his job.

Jerry looked at his watch. He had a little while before his briefing—just enough time to make a quick trip to eighty-two to touch base with his staff—and maybe grab some coffee from the meeting room. Leaving his office, Jerry took the elevator to the eighty-second floor.

8:12 A.M.

Sonia Henriquez had been catnapping, and when she opened her eyes she realized the bus was still in the Lincoln Tunnel. *Why is it taking so long to get through this traffic?* she asked herself. After punching the snooze alarm a few times too many, this delay now added to her anxiety. She did not want to arrive late.

Soothing her anxiety, she retreated into the wonderful memories of her recent fun-filled Royal Caribbean Cruise with her cousins, and visions of adventure began circulating through her mind. She closed her eyes to catch another few minutes' sleep before the bus arrived at the Port Authority Bus Terminal at Forty-Second Street and Eighth Avenue and her transfer to the downtown E-train.

###

8:15 A.M.

It was a fine day as Mike Craparo made his way from his home in Yonkers, New York, threading his way through the intricacies of the New York City transportation system. He finally exited the Lexington Avenue number-six train, ascending to Dey Street.

Looking up at those gigantic monuments to mankind's engineering genius, set against the clear, blue day, he reflected that it was only a year and a half ago that, after thirty-two years, he had retired as the chief of police of the Mount Vernon, New York, force. And now he was in his second year employed by Summit Securities, managing the seventy-five guards that operated the World Trade Center's four visitor desks.

Walking through the five-acre plaza, he decided to skip the normal trip to his office on the thirty-fifth floor of Tower Two, and go directly to the visitor desk on the north side of the lobby of Tower One. *I love this job*, Mike thought as he navigated through the thousands of commuters keeping the wheels of commerce rolling, each converging from all points in the tri-state area into downtown Manhattan.

"Good morning, Amanda. Good morning, Jamie," he greeted as he went down the line making personal contact with each of the fifteen "visitor greeters" on duty for the morning shift.

Over thirty-five thousand visitors each day passed through the World Trade Center. And each one had to be processed through the recently installed visitor security system. It was a facet of the hardening of the facility after the February 1993 bombing. Everything possible was being done to thwart another terrorist attempt.

This was a heady job.

###

8:30 A.M.

Since 6:30 a.m., Jim Usher had been in his office on the B-1 level—one of the six basements—of the South Tower, Tower Two. He was managing director in charge of installing the new fiber-optic signal repeater system in the Twin Towers. It was his habit to arrive early to assess the progress of his project, and juggle the myriad priorities for the coming day.

Jim was an anomaly; to know him, he was better suited on a horse in Wyoming than in his Brooks Brothers suit sitting behind a desk in New York City. At six foot three, and 210 pounds of solid muscle, he was a ruggedly handsome man who sported a neatly trimmed blond mustache and conservatively styled blond hair. He put the Marlboro Man to shame. A single parent, at age forty-eight his active social calendar almost required the services of a social secretary to prevent duplicate bookings.

"Roger," Jim asked his associate, "have we got all the information we need for our nine o'clock meeting with engineering?" Engineering was their client and a demanding customer. They had to be; they'd lived through and suffered the February 26, 1993, bombing of the World Trade Center, and every effort was being made not to allow a repeat performance of that tragedy. Jim and his firm were a key component in that effort.

Gabriella Ballini, a structural engineer for eleven years with the Port Authority, had a bad case of neurodermatitis, or eczema, which frequently flared up from insect bites or contact with poisonous plants. She was on the eighty-second floor of Tower One preparing for the regular Tuesday staff meeting when her boss, Jerry Dinkels, approached her.

Jerry took one look at Gabriella's arms and said, "Ah, Gabriella, you've got to take care of yourself." Gabriella was always landscaping and doing things around her New Jersey home adjacent to the Pine Barrens.

"I just don't learn, Jerry," Gabriella said. She never properly covered up and got bitten by insects and exposed to poison sumac every year.

"Look," Jerry said, "Why don't you go down to Duane Reade in the mall before the meeting and get something for that? I have to run down and brief Achille now, so I'll see you at our nine o'clock meeting."

"Okay, Jerry. See you there," Gabriella replied, getting up to head toward the elevators. However, she was intercepted by other staff members who began to drift toward the meeting room on the west side of the floor where breakfast was also being served, and they began to talk.

###

8:42 A.M.

Her bus finally having made it through the Lincoln Tunnel, Sonia Henriquez transferred to the subway for the final leg downtown. Getting off the E-train at the last stop, Chambers Street, World Trade Center, Sonia looked at her watch. *Oh, Lord,* she exclaimed to herself, *it's 8:42 and I'm late!* Adjusting her backpack and picking up her pace, she assumed that walk all New Yorkers take on rushing to work, and made her way like a broken-field runner through the crowded five-acre mall to Tower One.

Half walking, half running toward the elevators in Tower One, the aroma from the coffee station just outside the revolving doors stopped Sonia in her tracks. She had already had her morning cup of coffee at home, and for the past three months had been trying to cut down on her caffeine intake, going directly to her office on the sixty-eighth floor.

But this morning something made her think to herself, *Don't deprive yourself of coffee. Go have it!* Five seconds from the revolving doors and the elevators, Sonia made a quick right, readjusted her backpack, and stood third in line.

###

8:45 A.M.

Becoming engaged in conversation, and not wishing to miss the best part of Jerry Dinkels's weekly meeting—breakfast—Gabriella Ballini made a decision at the same time the elevator bell announced its arrival. *You know what?* she thought to herself. *I'll go down to Duane Reade after the meeting.* And she turned and walked back toward the meeting room on the eighty-second floor.

###

"Good morning, Sam," Tad Hanc said cheerfully to his coworker, Sam Sharma, as he got up from his desk and began collecting the items he required for a 9:00 a.m. final inspection of equipment installed on the

B-6 level. The B-6 level was the lowest level of six basements eighty feet below the main lobby. After collecting his flashlight, keys to open doors, and the project folder, Tad looked out his eighty-sixth-floor windows, taking a moment to absorb the beautiful view of upper Manhattan before heading into the bowels of Tower One. The Hudson River to his left and East River to the right were silvery ribbons reflecting the morning sunlight. Because of the exceptional clarity of the day, he could see north beyond the Bronx and into Westchester County. And on a really clear day like today, because he knew exactly where to look, maybe he'd be lucky enough to see the speck of an aircraft landing or taking off at the Westchester County Airport north of White Plains about twenty-nine miles distant.

Shifting his weight to the ball of his foot to turn and make his way to the inspection, out of the corner of his eye he registered that there was something wrong.

The view . . . *there is something not right, out-of-order, about the view,* Tad noticed. Turning back, studying the skyline, he began to take it in. At any given time a dozen aircraft could be seen flying over Manhattan: helicopter tours up and down both rivers, commuter flights going up the Hudson to Westchester County Airport, passenger jets cutting across the city to LaGuardia Airport's Runway 13. But . . . *this is different,* his brain was telling him. And then it registered—in all its horrifying aspects.

Lowering his eyes slightly, a thousand feet above the sidewalks of Manhattanites hustling and bustling to their places of business, Tad saw a large passenger airliner heading due south, just missing the top of the Empire State Building, flying very, very fast—heading straight toward Tower One.

###

Back in the groove after four days off, Nancy Seliga felt ready for her weekly Tuesday building managers meeting, which was just about to get started. Nancy had made the coffee earlier, and the croissants and bagels were set out on the table. Everyone was getting seated; Nancy had taken her regular spot facing inward, her back to the north windows on the twenty-first floor of the North Tower. She carefully placed her coffee mug in its designated spot on the conference table. "Delicious," she said to no one in particular after taking a sip, wiping the corners of her mouth and distorting her beautiful smile with the thumb and forefinger of her left hand. "Shall we get started?"

Tad Hanc continued to stare at that jet, thinking fast as it flew at over five hundred miles per hour directly at the tower. *It must be engine trouble or some other mechanical problem,* Tad figured, looking to see if there was any smoke trail coming out from behind the aircraft. But he saw nothing that indicated mechanical troubles and concluded that it must be a pilot problem. Mesmerized by the rapidly unfolding event, both curious and perplexed at an aircraft flying so low over Manhattan, Tad hoped that the pilot was taking corrective action, doing everything possible to steer the aircraft away from the tower.

As he stood, frozen, looking out his window, he realized that the plane was flying not only toward the tower, but that it was approaching very, very fast—aiming directly toward his window—directly at him!

###

"Charlie!" Jim Usher exclaimed, surprised to see him walking into the office. "What are you doing down here?"

Charlie had been on the 108th floor of Tower One repairing an emergency digital transfer relay switch on the new fiber-optic signal repeater system Jim's company was installing. When he discovered that he needed a part, he picked up his new two-way radio to ask an associate to bring it up. But the radio was dead! So he had to go to all the inconvenience and trouble of locking the electrical relay room door, walking down to the 107th floor, taking the local elevator to the seventy-eighth-floor sky lobby, transferring to the express elevator to the main lobby, hiking through the mall, going down the stairwell behind Ben & Jerry's, and walking through the maze of the B-1 level of the South Tower to the office to get a lousy ten-cent part that someone could have brought up to him.

Life was damned inconvenient at times, he thought, annoyed.

###

Helena Marietta had just swiped her WTC access ID card through a turnstile in the main lobby of the North Tower, and was standing in the center of the express elevator headed up to the seventy-eighth-floor sky lobby. Growing up on her daddy's horse ranch in Montana, she had always wanted to work in the Twin Towers.

After graduating high school, Helena had gone to secretarial school. At her request and to her delight the school placed her with a large financial services firm headquartered on the upper floors of the North Tower. She'd been with the firm for eight months now, and the commute was routine. Helena had been out late with her boyfriend the night before and she was running a few minutes late. She stood with her eyes closed, blocking out all the other passengers. *Just one more minute of peace and quiet,* she thought.

She marveled at how quickly the elevator rose, evidenced by the slight pressure in the soles of her feet, the pressure building in her ears, and the faint whooshing sound of air flowing past the cab. It was all very peaceful.

###

In the last instant that Tad Hanc knew he had left on this earth, watching that big airliner aimed directly at his window—directly at him—he saw the nose of the aircraft raise slightly, turning faintly to the east. And in that same moment he noticed the silhouettes of the pilots in the cockpit and of passengers in the windows. As the plane disappeared, Tad saw the American Airlines logo on the starboard side.

###

Captain Whitaker, still at his post in the mall, continued greeting those who walked by with "Hello" or "How are you?" as they cut the corner toward the South Tower or headed to the Marriott Hotel through the main lobby of Tower One.

Through the normal daily clamor of the mall of the World Trade Center, a sound like none other registered on the fringes of Tony's consciousness.

III

IMPACT

8:46 A.M.

The sound was that of a car crashing into an obstacle—the noise of glass and metal, only much, much louder. The tower shook violently, pushing south; then it came back. Tad Hanc didn't need to be a civil engineer, which he was, to know that the tower was ten feet out of plumb. He could see the plaza sidewalk abutting the tower wall a thousand feet down. He thought the building was going to snap, so out of plumb it was. As it swung back north, he thought it would stop; however, three more times the tower continued to swing—back and forth, back and forth, back and forth.

Jesus Christ! This is just an accident. Something very, very bad, but an accident, Tad silently exclaimed to himself. When the tower began to swing, in his mind he thought the aircraft had only clipped the corner of the building. Looking out the windows, he saw the debris—lots of debris falling down past his windows.

Pulling his eyes away from the falling debris, he turned to survey the office. Aside from a few ceiling tiles that had fallen, everything was working: the lights, air conditioning, telephones, computers . . .

Everything is working, Tad thought. *There can't be much damage to the building.* There was no panic on the floor as there were only two other employees present; it was still too early for the normal workday to begin. His heart beating a little more quickly than normal, Tad's calm, rational engineering mind was already calculating that repairs to the tower would take only a week or so to accomplish. That was his goal.

"What happened?" his two associates began shouting.

"What happened?" Tad parroted. "Oh, the plane just hit the building," he said a little too calmly.

"Oh, you're kidding, you're kidding?" someone else asked a little hysterically.

Sitting down at his desk, picking up the telephone to call his wife, Tad replied, "Yes."

Helena Marietta's peaceful tranquility riding up to the seventy-eighth-floor sky lobby turned into an instant living nightmare. The sudden explosion punched the elevator, forcing it down the shaft, and Helena found herself bouncing around the cab like a pinball, tumbling off the walls and crashing against everyone else.

She didn't know if she was awake, or asleep having a very bad dream. The explosion increased. She was flying, bouncing off the walls and other people. The heat was that of a blast furnace, and was accompanied by the thick, sickly smell of gasoline. The elevator was accelerating, banging recklessly down the shaft. The cab began to vibrate as the screeching sound of the emergency brakes tried to halt the plummet. There was another sound: screaming! She was screaming. Everyone was screaming! Between the screaming, screeching brakes, unbearable heat, and the smell, she couldn't breathe. And she couldn't comprehend the orange inferno melding through the top of the elevator. After what felt like an eternity, everyone crashed to the floor in a tumbled mass of tangled legs and arms as the elevator came to a loud, earsplitting, abrupt stop.

"What was that!?" Mike Craparo exclaimed aloud to himself. He was managing the North Tower's visitor desk and had just heard a muffled explosion, immediately followed by a shuddering in the whole tower. The trembling was so severe, Mike's first thought was that it was an earthquake, and his fear was that the marble walls against which he was standing were going to shatter and come crashing down upon him and all his visitor greeters.

"What is that?" he called out again, hearing a loud, whooshing sound coming from the twelve express elevators to the seventy-eighth-floor sky lobby. The reverberation became more strident with each passing instant.

"Everyone, get under the desk!" he yelled to his fifteen visitor greeters. Heart pounding, diving under the narrow marble desk for protection from God knows what, Mike heard the elevators crashing into the pits with the simultaneous explosions of enormous fireballs bursting through the highly polished, twelve-foot-high aluminum elevator doors. Mike was squished under the confines of the visitor desk, competing for space with Sam and Amanda, the computer CPUs, printer paper, UPS packages, duplex outlets, keyboard trays, and cables tangling themselves like writhing serpents. But none of that mattered. It was protection that he sought.

Suddenly he felt a tremendous, tortuous heat pass over him. He forced his eyes over his contorted body and that of Sam or Amanda, and he looked up. Out of the corner of his eye, he saw a colossal red-and-orange, scorching fireball bounce off the marble wall directly above them, rebounding toward the revolving doors that led to the five-acre mall that connected to the other buildings of the World Trade Center complex. The toxic smell of jet fuel was thick in the air.

Mike quickly extracted himself from under the visitor desk. "Everybody, get out!" he commanded, going down the line making contact with each person. "Get out and go over the North Bridge," he yelled. Mike was referring to the enclosed, elevated bridge over West Street that connected the World Trade Center's North Tower with the World Financial Center's Winter Garden.

Running through the portholes to the escalators leading up toward the bridge, looking over his left shoulder he could see half a dozen fireballs terrorizing pedestrians in the lobby.

Mike was no stranger to stress and danger. He had been involved in dozens of life-threatening situations over his thirty-two years in the police department, and before that as a Seabee in the Navy stationed in the Pacific. But this . . . this was encroaching upon the edge of sanity, his experience—and believability.

Postponing her elevator trip down to Duane Reade, Gabriella Ballini was on the eighty-second floor, swapping home remedies for poison sumac with another colleague while waiting for her meeting to begin.

"I just don't learn—" she began.

In that instant Gabriella was attacked by deafening thunderclaps and a bolt of lightning from above, accompanied by static, wind, a mist of smoke—and a terrible vibration in the floor. The tower took a leap, twisting, accelerating, distorting south, then rotating north, and bending back south again. Then it bent north, settling.

Gabriella hung on for dear life, her ears ringing from that most incredible sound while she tried to take a breath through the mist and smoke. Loose objects fell to the floor along with a colleague whose shoes had somehow separated from her feet. In that same split-second, Gabriella's view west outside the tower disappeared into a fusillade of flying, falling, whirling paper and wreckage. In that same instant, while she couldn't be sure of anything at this point, she thought she saw . . . things . . . bodies? . . . falling down outside the windows.

In total disbelief and shock, surprised the tower hadn't fallen down, butterflies in her stomach, Gabriella thought to herself, *We've got to get out of here!* She checked to see that she wasn't dreaming and was still alive. *My gosh! This building*—her worried engineer's mind analyzed—*bent ten feet!* It must have been an airplane, she concluded.

People everywhere were jumping up, running, and screaming, "Get out of the building!" Gabriella saw her two bosses, Greg Reszka and Al Simmons, run from their offices on the northeast side of the floor, yelling, "Out of the building!" From above, she heard clanking, crashing sounds, which impelled her to action.

Obeying—as if they needed permission—everyone immediately ran to the nearest of three stairwells in the core of the floor. Denise Berger left so fast she jumped right out of her shoes, running barefoot. Gabriella bent, like a polo player hitting the ball, never breaking stride, and retrieved the deserted footwear. People began crying in the fast-filling smoky floor, and Gabriella could see the fear in their eyes and realized that she too must look that way to them. And in that same moment of horror, she realized that there was a real possibility that she would never see Neil, her wonderful husband and soul mate, and their three beautiful children, Kristen, Carlo, and feisty little Glenda, again. This realization, more than anything else happening in this nightmarish morning, filled her with dread—and a determination to escape.

"What was that?" Jim Usher's baritone voice demanded. From his basement B-1 level office, he had felt in his bones, rather than heard, a muffled sound, something like an explosion way off in the distance. It was a subtle assault on the ears . . . an increase in air pressure. The whole experience, though only a second in length, was unnerving. As he looked around the office, he saw that the others had noticed it too. Something—he didn't know what—was out of place. Something was drastically wrong.

"One medium regular coffee, please," Sonia Henriquez ordered from the server behind the coffee station counter.

Watching the crowds of people as she waited, she noticed that the other two women who had been in line ahead of her had passed through the revolving doors into the main lobby of Tower One. Sonia's coffee was delivered to the counter, and as she reached into her pocketbook for change, suddenly there was a huge commotion coming from inside the main lobby. As she turned her head left to see what was happening, she saw hundreds of people in the lobby screaming, running back through the revolving doors, tripping over each other in the turmoil.

In all her years working at the World Trade Center, Sonia had never seen the doors spin so fast; two, three people crammed into the little space, all trying to jam through at the same time.

She stood, mesmerized, unable to pull her eyes off the mayhem. *Oh, my God!* she thought. *Is there a shooter in the lobby?* That was her first thought. What else could explain such panic? It had to be a shooter. Instead of running, Sonia just stood there and watched, stunned.

Without warning, there was a massive explosion and a huge ball of fire came crashing from the elevator shaft, blowing through the revolving doors out to the mall. The pressure from the explosion knocked people to the floor, and people tripped over each other in the panic, falling. Those in the fireball's path were instantly ignited like an emergency road flare.

Instinctively Sonia grabbed her backpack and pulled it in front of her body as she scampered and backed into the little cubbyhole space between the cash register and the condiment station. Another fireball roared through the glass partition separating the lobby from the mall, and bounced off the mirror over the coffee station, which exploded and crashed to the floor, badly burning and cutting the employees behind the counter.

Miraculously, the fireball ricocheted ten feet away from Sonia—but the heat! The heat felt like when you're baking cookies and you stick your face in the oven as you open the door. Whoosh!

And in an instant, it was over.

On the eighty-sixth floor, Yvonne Barker had just hung up the phone after a brief conversation with her sister-in-law, discussing the upcoming wedding trip to the islands, when suddenly the tower began shaking like someone going into convulsions. Yvonne heard loud crashing at the entrance to the office. She jerked her head in that direction and saw the ceiling and everything around it falling. Stuff just kept falling through the ceiling.

Yvonne started screaming. Self-preservation and survival instinct took over, and she dived under her desk. Then, as quickly as it began—the spasmodic shaking and thunderous crashing of debris through the ceiling—it ended. Yvonne was crying when Flory hurried over to her station.

"I think a plane just hit the building," he announced, making it a statement of fact.

"What!?" Yvonne was hysterical now.

"We're going to get out of here!" Flory stated emphatically, grabbing her hand. "We're going to get out of here!"

Flory half dragged Yvonne by the hand to the entrance of the office. But it was totally blocked by ceiling debris, sheetrock, large chunks of jagged concrete, and metal. Looking up, there was a huge hole in the ceiling: the floor of eighty-seven. Yvonne looked below—that hole went all the way down! The lights had remained on, so it was easy to see the devastation, and the floor below.

"Be careful. Don't slip," Flory calmly cautioned.

Together, Yvonne and Flory worked with their bare hands to clear the debris blocking the doorway, their only way out of the office space to get to the stairwells. Grunting and groaning, they finally managed to make a hole just large enough for them to squeeze through.

Afraid and shaking, Yvonne practically ran through the adjacent office to the door leading into the core of the tower. Together, she and Flory opened the door. There was nothing but blackness—and there was smoke.

Vic Guarnera had just returned from the 107th floor of Tower Two, testing the security doors on the observation deck. When he exited the elevator onto the thirty-fifth floor of the South Tower, he met Doug Karpiloff and a few other people. As they began to discuss what their morning itinerary was going to be, the speakers on all their two-way radios virtually exploded with the screaming voice of Jonesie, one of Vic's staff in the Security Command Center. The terrified sound of her voice galvanized everyone to immediate action.

Jonesie was the security officer in charge of the eight-to-four shift in the Security Command Center on the twenty-second floor of the North Tower. She controlled the hundreds of security cameras throughout the World Trade Center complex as well as access through the 108 turnstiles and two thousand security doors. Her responsibilities were considerable. She had the disposition to carry out her job calmly and dispassionately and had never been known to raise her voice.

"We've just been hit by a plane!" she screamed hysterically. "There's debris . . . and everything . . . falling everywhere! People are falling past our windows!" Jonesie screamed. She sounded terrified.

As soon as the channel cleared, Vic pushed the transmit button. "Are you okay?" he asked.

"Yes," was her terrified reply.

"I'm on my way," Vic informed her. "Just try to calm down and see what you can do. Make sure that the system is working well. I'll be there as soon as possible," he said quietly, attempting to help calm her.

Doug Karpiloff, Vic's boss, was standing next to him and had heard everything. Eddie Strauss and John O'Neill were present, as well as some other operational folks. Jonesie's frantic outburst was enough to impel them all to immediate action, as they responded to their various command desks. Doug instructed Vic to go to the Security Command Center on the twenty-second floor of Tower One, while he left for the Fire Command Desk in Tower One's main lobby.

His quick briefing to his boss, Achille, completed, Jerry Dinkels asked if he could go see the chief engineer, Frank Lombardi, about a couple of other unrelated matters that required clarification. "Then I've got to get upstairs to my meeting," he said. "I don't want to be late."

"Sure, not a problem," Achille agreed.

Jerry placed his hands on the arms of the guest chair in Achille's seventy-second-floor office, and began lifting himself out of the seat to go and speak with Frank. At the point of least stability, Jerry was thrown out of the chair. There was a violent impact immediately followed by an explosion, and the tower began to sway and deflect. The sound of women screaming came from the outside offices as Jerry regained his balance.

"What was that?" Jerry and Achille asked, looking at each other, bewildered, not knowing what was happening.

Looking out of Achille's southwest office windows, Jerry suddenly saw burning papers raining down from above.

"Everyone get away from the windows!" Jerry instructed forcefully. His first thought was that a small plane, a Cessna, or perhaps a helicopter had hit the tower. Then, seeing all the paper, it flashed through his mind that this was a terrorist attack and that they were throwing propaganda leaflets down. But then he saw a *Time* magazine floating down past the window.

Nah! Jerry concluded. *There's no one throwing* Time *magazines at us.*

"Everybody go!" he commanded. "Everybody out of the office!"

Jerry was concerned about his staff on the eighty-second floor. He attempted calling them but nobody answered the phone. Turning to Jack Spencer he said, "Jack, I'm going up to eighty-two to check on my staff. I'll be right back."

The nearest stairway was the C-stairwell on the west side of the tower. The seventy-second floor was a non-entry floor—the doors were locked and couldn't be opened from the stairwell, so Jerry unrolled some of the fire hose from its spindle and wrapped it around the doorknob to prevent it from closing. He didn't want to be locked out when he returned with his staff.

Walking quickly up the steps, by the time he reached the seventy-fourth floor, the strong smell of jet fuel invaded his nostrils. There was haze but no smoke.

This is not good! he thought.

Suddenly, walking up wasn't such a good idea, so he turned around and returned to the seventy-second floor, curious as to why he hadn't seen anyone in the stairwell. Unwrapping the fire hose, letting the door close, Jerry heard lots of noise—people shouting as they began to go down the stairwell. And alarm bells.

Jerry reentered the office space and noticed that Frank Lombardi was still in his corner office.

"Frank," he called out, "we gotta go!" Then he walked the perimeter of the entire floor to ensure that everyone had evacuated. Once he returned to the core of the building, he again heard alarm bells and realized that it was the elevator alarm . . . the one that rings when that big red button is pushed.

###

Police Officer David Lim and his K-9 partner, Sirius, were in the kennels on the B-1 level, the first of six basement levels under the South Tower.

The sound was distant thunder, muffled. He felt it in his bones. There was no doubt in David's trained and disciplined mind that what he felt and heard was caused by an explosion. Confirmation came quickly; he received a call on his radio that there had been an explosion high in the North Tower.

"8-13" David heard. The code for *assist police officer*. This code was serious. It was used only to summon all officers immediately to a location to assist in an emergency.

"One must have gotten by us," he commented with resignation to Sirius.

Since an explosion had obviously occurred, Officer Lim didn't require the services of his explosive-sniffing K-9. He gave the command to his partner, Sirius, to enter his personal kennel-habitat, and threw the latch.

"You stay there," he instructed his faithful friend and partner of almost two years. "I'll be back for you," he promised.

Officer Lim walked with quick determination through the labyrinth of the sub-basement, took the stairs by the ID Badging Office, and exited next to Ben & Jerry's in the mall, just adjacent to the main lobby of the South Tower, Tower Two. He sprinted the two hundred or so feet through the remarkably empty mall, passed through the center revolving doors into the main lobby of Tower One, and took the escalator steps two at a time until he reached the mezzanine overlooking the plaza.

The plaza was a favorite gathering and meeting place for colleagues during lunch. It was five acres of park-like space with trees and benches between the four main World Trade Center buildings. Anchoring its center was a beautiful large circular fountain with a modern Atlas bearing the weight of the earth on his shoulders. In the summer months, music filled the plaza as outdoor concerts were performed at the base of Tower One. It was a peaceful area to escape the heavy responsibilities and pressures of business.

"What the hell!" he exclaimed to himself in Chinese. The sight was totally unexpected. There was a full-scale blizzard of paper, magazines, boxes . . . and chunks of metal imbedded in the recently refurbished plaza terrazzo.

People were pouring out of the A and C stairwells. David was a cop so he began directing them down the escalator, advising them to exit through the mall at either Vesey or Church Street.

"Officer?" It was a civilian tapping him on the shoulder, trying to get his attention. "Officer," he said with more determination, "there's a body lying in the plaza." David turned and looked where the civilian was pointing, toward the stage.

"What the hell!" he exclaimed again, shocked, staring at what looked like a body about twenty feet away, crumpled at the base of Tower One. David raced through the doors into the plaza and ran to the body. It was a man. *This man either jumped or was thrown out from one of the upper floors*, he reasoned. *Regardless, he's dead!*

In all his years on the force, he had never seen anything like this. He wasn't just "dead." His whole body was distorted, as if all the bones were broken . . . and there was lots of blood. Calling in the dead on arrival, the DOA, was now his new priority—his most important job. As he pulled the radio from his belt, what sounded like a 12-gauge shotgun blasted behind him. Startled, he quickly turned, radio to his mouth, and saw a new body lying in the plaza not fifty feet away.

Oh, my God! he thought. *There's got to be other things going on up there.* David's radio crackled to life, with the assist police officer code: "8-13. Multiple aided on the upper floors. All units respond."

Just then, Port Authority Police Officer David Lim looked straight up . . .

###

Nancy Seliga's meeting never happened. She had just placed her coffee cup down when she heard a tremendous explosion from high in the tower. The tower rocked, shaking violently. Bern D'Leo, who was walking around the table distributing a report, was thrown to the floor. One of the contractors from ABM building maintenance and facility services dived under the table.

Nancy twisted around in her chair to look out the windows and what she saw was totally unexpected. Standing, she stepped closer to the windows, mesmerized by the falling debris, paper, and chunks of metal. "Is that part of the building?" she asked aloud. In complete terror, her staff was screaming at her to get away from the windows.

"Oh, my God!" she exclaimed.

Nancy considered herself a good Catholic, but there were times when extenuating circumstances warranted a right and proper expletive. Today had turned into one of those times.

"Oh, my God—!" she exclaimed again, not completing her sentence, fearing that what she thought she just saw falling past her window might be accurate.

In that same instant, turning her head to look back into the room, she and Bob Benacchio made eye contact and, as if previously rehearsed, said in unison, "It's a plane!"

Awestruck, Nancy turned back to the windows.

"Nancy!" Bob yelled. "We have *got* to get out of here and down to the Fire Command Desk!" When she didn't immediately respond, Bob yelled again, "Nan-cy!" emphasizing both syllables, "We've got to get out of here! Hurry up!"

She'd seen enough and knew it was time. Bob had brought her attention back to reality. There was work to do this day.

###

Ed Bonny was driving the Port Authority car out of the underground parking area to go to the security meeting on Staten Island; John Fisher was riding shotgun. Ed approached the Prox-card reader on the B-1 level that signaled to raise the rolling door, allowing them to exit the building up the ramp and out onto West Street.

"Did you hear that?" John asked, suddenly alert to an anomaly in the building. "What was that?"

"What are you talking about, John?" Ed replied. "I didn't hear anything."

"It was more of a feeling . . . a pressure change, something—"

"I didn't feel anything, John," Ed said, interrupting, as the rolling door went into motion and began winding up. When it had risen sufficiently to allow the car through, Ed put it into gear and began to drive slowly up the ramp.

"What the hell—!" Ed exclaimed, braking the car to a stop short of the Delta-barrier. Garbage was hailing out of the sky down upon them. Shrapnel and chunks of metal hit the roof, pummeling the car. And paper! There was paper all over the place, and burning paper floated down all around. Ed and John had just driven out from sanity, into insanity!

Unsnapping his seatbelt, Ed wanted to get out of the car for a better look—to see what was causing this nightmare. As he reached for the latch to open the door, John reached over and grabbed his arm.

"Don't get out of the car!" John demanded.

"Why?" Ed challenged.

Ed had been in the Marine Corps, deployed to Vietnam in the early sixties, training Guerrillas. He knew about shrapnel.

They both sat, absolutely dumbfounded at what was happening around them. When the pelting of shrapnel stopped, they both got out of the car and looked up. They were just a little north of the north face of Tower One, and from that vantage point, both concluded that an explosion had occurred at about the eighty-eighth floor—the Silverstein floor. Ed instantly knew it was terrorists, because there was nothing in the building that could blow up like that.

"Ah . . . in six months we could fix this," Ed stated, referring to the apparent damage.

"My thoughts, exactly," John confirmed. John and Ed, though both consultants, like the men and women that ran the towers had a loyalty and devotion to them that transcended all else. And their first thoughts were to the safety, security, and well-being of the tenants—and the towers.

Ed's mind was crystal clear as he began laying out a plan of action. "Staten Island's out," he stated. "We can't go back into the towers, John. We have to go to New Jersey to set up a communications center."

"No," John objected. "I gotta go back into the towers!"

"John!" Ed stated with emphasis. "You lost! The terrorists won. Somehow they got the damn bomb in the building. We've got to start all over again at square one." Ed was referring to the Permanent Security Program, an access control system to prevent the repeat of the '93 bombing. The past five years, both Ed and John—working closely with Doug Karpiloff—were instrumental in the installation and implementation of the security upgrade for the World Trade Center.

"We'll go over to New Jersey and do all the things I said," Ed re-emphasized.

"No!" John repeated emphatically, angrily. "I have got to go back into the building to the OCC. It's mine!" John stated categorically, claiming ownership—and responsibility—of the Operations Command Center in the basement of the South Tower. No one knew the systems in the OCC better than John Fisher. He had specified them, and he had been there every step of the way during installation and testing. He knew he would be of service in *his* OCC.

"Okay," Ed acquiesced. He wasn't John's boss and didn't have the authority to order him not to go. They were colleagues, and John was free to do whatever he thought best. "Get in the car. I'll drive you there," Ed said, and they both got back into the car.

The anti-terrorist vehicle barrier, the Delta-barrier, remained in the closed position. Ed swiped his Prox-card over the reader to let the guard know he was authorized to lower the barrier. When nothing happened, Ed looked back at the guard in the booth. What he saw was an utterly thunderstruck guard locked in the booth, in complete shock. Ed finally got his attention by leaning on the horn and signaling him to lower the barrier.

When Ed drove over the barrier and onto West Street, the horror of the beautiful day that had turned into a nightmare magnified exponentially. Ed saw at least two dozen bodies sprawled all over West Street—some as far as the middle of the road. There was broken glass all over the place, and mixed in with metal and tons of paper was blood. He tried to fathom whether these people were blown out of the tower with the explosion, or killed with the metal, shrapnel, and debris—or both. One lady off to his right was definitely a victim of shrapnel; someone was trying to administer first aid, and there were shards sticking out all over her.

Ed was immediately concerned for his wife, Pat, up on the sixty-first floor. Pat was a survivor. She had commanded great respect from those with whom she had evacuated during the 1993 bombing. Ed knew she would do well today. He also knew that he couldn't stay there to wait for her because there were a hundred ways to exit the buildings. *I'd never be able to find her*, he correctly reasoned. He knew Pat would acquit herself well, and find her way safely home.

Ed made an illegal U-turn, careful not to drive over any bodies, and got as close to the lobby of Tower One as he could.

"How the hell did all this happen?" he asked rhetorically, observing the burnt and scorched front of the lobby, and blown-out plateglass windows.

Without a word, John reached back to the rear seat, dragged out his brown leather briefcase, opened the passenger door, and jumped out. He quickly walked through the debris and past the bodies, briefcase in his left hand, and disappeared in his green, sharkskin suit into the interior of the main lobby, heading to the OCC in the B-1 basement level of Tower Two.

John was going into his element. Ed turned the car north on West Street, drove through an empty Holland Tunnel to the Port Authority Technical Center in Jersey City, New Jersey, to carry out his plan to establish a communication center.

Checking his watch, Erik Ronningen made a mental note that his colleague Nuri Hamidi, normally in at 8:30 a.m., and his boss, Bob Bernard, had yet to arrive at the office. *They're probably in the elevator*, he thought. From past experience Erik knew that when they were late, they usually arrived at about this time. He continued to prepare for his nine o'clock meeting scheduled in the upper floors of the North Tower.

Suddenly and without warning the entire tower jolted south, twisting, similar to being punched off-center by a giant fist. It then snapped north, wrenched back again, and yet again, staggering like a boxer dazed from a right-cross punch and struggling to regain his balance. People walking or standing were thrown to the floor while the rest hung on to whatever was convenient, for dear life.

The accompanying roar from somewhere above assaulted Erik's ears and sounded like a hundred express freight trains crossing an old railroad trestle. Sitting not three feet from the windows, he kicked back his desk chair and rolled out of his cubicle into the open area.

My God!, he thought. *This building is going to snap and pitch over like an extension ladder.* Erik looked up in anticipation of the floors above raining down upon him, and hunched down in a position of self-preservation hoping to protect his head and body from the collapsing ceiling. Quickly chiding himself that no amount of hunching would protect him—that he should sit up and die like a man—Erik stood up, looked out the windows, and watched a huge, flaming red-and-orange fireball come whooshing, blistering, down and explode not twenty-five feet outside his windows. Miraculously, the windows didn't shatter.

Then the blizzard began—a blizzard of falling paper, debris, and rubbish forced out of the upper tower from the explosion, resembling a midwinter, Great Plains storm. So intense was the raining wreckage that the beautiful view of New York Harbor could no longer be seen. A FedEx package came spiraling down in the mix and made Erik immediately think of the Tom Hanks' movie *Cast Away*. The mind is a curious mechanism.

Police Captain Tony Whitaker was outside the Banana Republic when a sound like none other registered on the fringes of his consciousness. Then he heard a strange roar somewhere off to his left. The unusual noise puzzled him as the sound continued to increase in volume, getting louder, exponentially louder, with each passing electronic tick on the LCD clock of his pager. In one electronic tick, he thought the malicious monstrous roar was standing next to him, rudely pushing his shoulder, pressing against the side of his face.

Tony snapped his head to the left and the sight horrified him. A mammoth, roaring fireball, searing red, orange, and blinding yellow—

something out of science fiction—burst from the doors of the express elevators to the forty-fourth floor, the forty-four-car side near the Marriott Hotel of the main lobby in Tower One, and passed through the walls containing the revolving doors as easily as a hot wind blowing across the Great Plains. In the same horrifying instant, Tony saw people being thrust in front of it, dragged into it from its periphery, and free-floating like pinwheels inside of it. And in that same horrifying tick of time, Tony had the awful realization that the giant, malicious, people-devouring fireball was roaring directly toward him!

Tony instantly went into action. Call it instinct, reflex—Tony hoped it was training—his 235-pound, six-foot-one-inch running back body was in motion. He didn't feel like he was in control, but his body was making all the right moves. Pivoting ninety degrees left, his legs were propelling him in the direction of the South Tower. As he ran, his arms were widespread, cross-like, gathering up people walking toward the North Tower, capturing them like fish in a net and dumping them eighty feet from his "image-spot," in a narrow access corridor leading to a freight elevator between the Banana Republic and Chase Bank.

In one heap they all tumbled. Tony didn't know how long he was there. Eventually he became aware that he was alone. It was dark; the smell of jet fuel filled his nostrils. Climbing to his knees, he began to feel about, patting himself down, checking to see if his body was serviceable.

"Thank God, it is," he said aloud with gratitude.

The image of that mammoth, people-consuming fireball was scorched into his memory. He clambered to his feet and dragged his body back out into the main corridor of the mall. It was dark. It was silent. Turning right, back toward the North Tower, Tony tripped on something soft and staggered like a drunk. He stepped on another soft object and instinctively knew what it was.

Don't look down, a little voice in his head instructed.

In the distance, he saw two bright, blazing images coming toward him from the general direction of the main lobby of the North Tower. As the images got closer, Tony realized with horror that they were two people on fire, running silently past him. It appeared as if their clothes had burned off and they were running naked, flaming.

As quickly as they came, they were gone.

IV

EVACUATION & ESCAPE

8:47 A.M.

"I gotta get out of here!" Sonia Henriquez said out loud to herself. She was in the towers during the February 1993 bombing and recalled that day; there was no question in her mind that the terrorists had attacked again. She knew it was a bomb and said, "They got us this time!"

Sonia unfolded herself from the little nook of protection at the coffee station, quickly slipped on her backpack, and turned left. She joined the swarms of running, panicking people in the mall and ran straight down toward Warner Brothers. When she reached the escalators on the left, she ran up them going toward the Borders bookstore and exited the building onto Church Street. Sonia never looked back as she made her way to safety, running up Fulton Street.

At this moment, being an engineer was working against Gabriella Ballini. Bolting toward the eighty-second-floor stairwell closest to her, she knew their office was nearly nine hundred feet above West Street. Being a structural engineer, she also knew it was a miracle that the building hadn't broken and fallen down. It was still standing—at the moment. Gabriella was thinking about transfer loads and questioning column connections. The building had twisted and bent ten feet, she figured, and the structural loads had to have equaled themselves out. *How were the trusses holding out?* she wondered, extremely nervous. Then she thought about her loving family and wondered if she'd ever see them again.

The tower had stopped its dizzying sway and was miraculously upright. The ceiling seemed to be holding its own, but the debris was raining down outside the windows at a furious rate. From all around the seventy-first-floor office, voices were yelling to evacuate the building. As Erik Ronningen turned away from the southerly exposure, still not certain that his eyes and ears were telling the truth, he saw a woman standing not three feet away, staring at him. "Whitney!" he exclaimed, not just a little surprised to see Whitney Birch. "What are you doing here?"

"Kylie couldn't make it today, Erik, so I took her place," she responded, referring to her associate from the consulting firm of Arthur Andersen.

Voices shouted from all around the square-acre floor, growing more urgent as smoke began to invade the premises from the elevator shafts and elsewhere: "Evacuate the building! Everyone get out of the building, now!"

"I'll escort you down the stairwell, Whitney," Erik offered, and concluded that there was only one logical answer that had caused this instant madness: an airplane had somehow, inexplicably driven into the upper portion of the tower.

8:48 A.M.

Sarah Ronningen, Erik's wife, had just arrived in her office, when the telephone rang. "Greenwich Association of Realtors, this is Sarah, how may I help you?" she cheerfully asked.

"Sarah, this is Diane," her associate Diane Ivey said with a sense of urgency. "An airplane has just hit the World Trade Center towers. I thought you ought to know. It looks like a terrorist attack."

"Thank you, Diane."

Sarah was not overly anxious. She understood how well the towers were built. Hanging up, she got up and turned on the radio and all the stations were reporting the incident. Concerned, but not very worried about what she heard, she called Erik at his office.

"Hi. This is Erik. I'm not able to take your call at the moment, so please leave your name and phone number at the sound of the tone, and I'll return your call. Thank you."

Damn, he's not answering, she thought.

Beep.

"Hi, love, it's me. I just heard on the radio about a plane hitting the World Trade Center. Call me when you get a chance. Bye."

Everything seemed normal. The phones were working, but she certainly didn't like the idea of a plane hitting a tower.

Jim Usher knew something was drastically wrong when he heard that muffled explosion. From his days in law enforcement, and with previous experience in a covert unit buried deep within the bureaucracy of the U.S. government, Jim's intuition told him that this situation was very serious.

"Everybody get out of the building!" Jim commanded. The sickening aroma of JP-4 jet fuel thickened the air. Rumors were that there had been an explosion in the North Tower, possibly even that an aircraft had accidentally hit the building.

"Roger, get off the phone and get out of the building, now!" Jim ordered. When his colleague didn't immediately comply, in three steps Jim was at his side, and with his large right hand grabbed the phone receiver from his ear, slammed it into its cradle, and with his other arm propelled him out of the office.

Jim then made a quick run around the B-1 level, telling everyone to evacuate the building. When he got to the key control room of the Operations Command Center, he told the guard behind the bulletproof glass to evacuate all personnel in the OCC.

"Mis', it's me," Tad Hanc said, calmly identifying himself to his wife, Grazyna, when she picked up after the first ring. Mis' was the pet nickname they had for each other. It meant "Little Bear" and was a term of endearment from their college days together in Poland in the '70s.

"A plane crashed into the building . . . but it's not too bad," he reported nonchalantly. "I'll be leaving soon, so not to worry, okay, Mis'?" Tad hung up, and noting that everything was working, he thought, *what the hell?*, and decided to e-mail his brother in Poland. In Polish he wrote, "A plane hit the building. I am fine. Don't worry. Everything is fine. I'll tell you more later."

Thinking back to the World Trade Center bombing of February 1993, he recalled that they were out of their offices for months and months, and that he wished he had taken some of his important items with him then.

Well, this time maybe I'll take some stuff I really need with me, he thought. *It may be a few weeks or even a month, but we will be coming back soon,* he convinced himself. Opening his briefcase and plopping it on the desk, Tad began going through his drawers, looking for personal papers and items he really needed. His mind began to race as he rummaged through the drawers, uncertain, not knowing what to take. "Ah, my flashlight," he said upon seeing it, tossing it into the case.

Closing his briefcase and shrugging into his suit jacket, he announced to his two coworkers, "Listen, guys. This is what I think. We are not going to be coming back that soon. You had better take some important stuff with you, too."

"No, no! Don't worry, Tad," they said. "Let's go! Let's go! We're going to be back soon. Don't worry about this stuff," they advised. "Just—let's go!" they repeated hurriedly.

8:49 A.M.

Helena Marietta was waking up. *What a frightening nightmare,* she thought. And then she came to the horrifying awareness that it was real. It was deathly quiet in the elevator. She was in a pile of people, and as they began to come to, they untangled their appendages and slowly got to their feet. No one said a word. They just looked around, dazed. Her skirt and blouse were torn, half-askew. Her face and hands felt singed like a sunburn after the first day at the beach. Her long, auburn hair was tangled like tumbleweed, and her high-heeled shoes were somewhere, not on her feet.

As people began to comprehend their plight, they began to panic. The emergency intercom wasn't working so they began to shout for help.

Silence was their only answer.

Gabriella Ballini ran down the stairs as fast as she could, thinking about the tower, nervous, still holding Denise's shoes in her hands. Her boss,

Greg Reszka, a six-foot-five big guy was in front. They reached the door on the seventy-sixth floor accessing the crossover. The crossover was a detour in the stairwell that took them around the two floors of mechanical equipment rooms before continuing down. The stairwell was smoky and Gabriella was nervous and perspiring profusely. Greg grasped the doorknob, twisting, pushing.

The door wouldn't budge.

Gabriella added her slight weight to Greg's, and others joined in to force the door open.

Nothing. The door wouldn't move. They might as well be trying to shove a granite mountain.

8:50 A.M.

"Everyone—turn around and go back up to the next access floor," Greg yelled. Gabriella Ballini and the others backed up, and the door on the seventy-seventh floor opened into the inspector general's office. Bob Van Etten, the inspector general, and Mike Nestor, the assistant inspector general, were there with their staff. And Myron Finegold and Vinny Borst from Office Space Services had convened from their offices on the eighty-second floor. Everyone was nervous, jumpy. Bob and Mike were trying to calm everyone.

Gabriella was perspiring more than was normal. She looked around and saw an old towel, a rag really, and snatched it up and began wiping her face with it.

Looking out the windows, Gabriella could see that a lot of things continued to fall out of the upper tower. She overheard someone speculating that a helicopter had hit the building. "What? Are you kidding me?" Gabriella responded.

Another said he saw that the top of the building was gone. *I guess they must have a television going in there*, Gabriella reasoned. Turning to Mike Nestor, she asked, "May I use the phone? I have to call my husband." Amazingly the telephones were still working.

"Neil, honey, it's me, Gabriella," she said, speaking to the answering machine. "Honey, I'm on the seventy-seventh floor. I'm not out yet. I think a plane hit the building and I'm trying to get down. I'll call you when I'm out. I love you . . . and the kids." And with that she hung up.

Walking over to Whitney's desk overlooking the east windows, Erik Ronningen saw that she was standing, hunched over her work surface, not moving. He looked out the windows and the debris continued to flood from the upper levels. Erik put his hand on Whitney Birch's shoulder and asked gently, "Are you okay?"

"Yeah, thanks, Erik. I'm fine," she responded calmly. "I'm just shutting down my laptop. I want to take it with me," she said, the epitome of control and composure in her voice.

The thought of the two CDs he made last week popped into Erik's head, so he turned away from Whitney and went to retrieve them. He had made a complete backup of all the documents and files for Bob Bernard's ongoing Newark Airport AirTrain electronic payment project. Erik pulled them out of his file drawer, grabbed his little black-fabric briefcase, and dropped them in. He then went back to Whitney's desk, briefcase in hand.

"Let's just do a quick walk-through to be sure everybody's out," Whitney suggested to him.

"Good idea."

Whitney picked up her laptop and they first checked to make sure that Bob Bernard and Nuri Hamidi were not in their offices. Confirming that they weren't, Whitney and Erik continued checking the remainder of the seventy-first floor. Everyone had left, and as they reached the core of the floor, Erik excused himself.

"Would you excuse me for a moment?" he asked Whitney, turning and entering the men's room. "I'll meet you at the stairs," he instructed before the door closed behind him. The twenty-ounce cup of coffee had had an hour and a half to work its way through his system. *It's going to be a long day*, Erik concluded.

As Sarah Ronningen settled in for her day's work, the phone rang a second time in as many minutes. "Hi, Sarah, it's Liz. I'm going to be over at Jackie's," she announced, a little concern betraying itself in her voice. Liz Kelly was Sarah's best friend, and Jackie was Doug Karpiloff's wife and long-time friend to both her and Erik.

"Thank you, Liz," Sarah responded, still not too concerned. "If anything comes up I'll let you know."

After hearing Jonesie's screaming voice over his two-way radio, Vic Guarnera took the elevator down to the main lobby from the thirty-fifth floor of the South Tower. The two-hundred-foot distance through the mall from the South to the North Tower—normally a studied disarray of activity as people bustled in from all the subway lines—was deserted and eerily quiet for morning rush hour.

All the lights were out except for the emergency lighting system, and as Vic approached the Banana Republic he noticed a couple of women straightening out clothing on the racks as they prepared to close and lock up. He also noticed that the huge directional signage was all twisted, bent, and partially hanging from the ceiling. The sprinkler system was in full sprinkle through the haze of smoke, and looking up, he was surprised to see a hole in the ceiling of the mall through to the plaza above. In his quest to get to the revolving doors, he had to run the gamut between the raining sprinkler heads in the hopes of remaining dry, but was not entirely successful.

People had just started emerging into the B-corridor from the stairwell. *Bank of America employees*, Vic thought, as he knew their offices started on the ninth floor. And now, on the mezzanine above the main lobby, people in various stages of distress and disarray, some without shoes, were beginning to come from stairwells A and C, and around down the escalator. Vic was standing at the bottom of the escalator and saw that the up escalator had been turned off, but the down side continued to operate.

Vic became aware of the sound of shattering glass. He turned and saw the glass above the revolving doors leading into the mall shatter, falling to the floor. He had the thought that the building was torquing, which would cause the glass to shatter. *Son-of-a-gun*, he thought.

People began to rush and panic, which brought Vic's attention back to the people squeezing onto the down escalator.

"Everyone, please remain calm," Vic instructed. "Remain calm and walk quickly," he called up to the folks rushing down. As they reached the bottom he further instructed, "Be careful, the floors are wet from the sprinklers."

As he was about to direct the people through the B-corridor and out of the tower onto West Street, Vic noticed that the west end of the B-corridor walls had collapsed into the corridor, and that there was debris everywhere. He had a flashback of his evacuation during the bombing in February 1993 and thought, *not again!*

Quickly adjusting to the circumstances, Vic directed everyone around the forty-four-car side—the express elevators to the forty-fourth floor—on the south side of the lobby, and out onto West Street. He figured that was where the fire department and the emergency units would be marshaling. So he sent people out that way for the fire department to handle triage and conduct traffic out of the tower.

"When do you think we'll get back in?" some folks asked Vic as they stepped off the bottom stair.

"Last time was two months," Vic replied. "We'll have to find out what the extent of the damage is and how long it is going to take us to repair it—and then we'll determine," he clarified. "We can't say anything right now." So they went on their way.

The firemen began entering the lobby looking for the stairwells, and Vic directed them in groups of five- and six-man teams toward the B-corridor stairwell. As he was about to follow them to go assist Jonesie, he noticed that the water was beginning to penetrate the motor pit of the escalators. No one listened, or heard his command to use the other escalator, so he ran up the stopped up escalator and directed people to go down the up side. But by habit, people were used to using the right inside escalator and didn't want to change. Vic had to physically stand in front of the down side to block them, and force them to go down the up side of the escalator. After the last person got off the down side, he turned it off. *At least now*, he figured, *I've prevented the potential for a fire.*

Vic never looked outside into the plaza.

###

8:51 A.M.

Rushing from her cancelled weekly meeting, Nancy Seliga returned to her office to grab her keys, pager, and radio . . . but overlooked her cell phone.

"Would you hurry up!?" her staff yelled at her.

"No! I gotta get my vest! I gotta get my vest!" she repeated. *Thank God for Doug*, she thought, referring to Doug Karpiloff, as she grabbed her emergency vest.

Doug knew his job and was tenacious about having the right equipment, and ensured that everyone was properly trained and drilled.

Thank God for Doug, she thought again as she left her office properly outfitted and trained, heading for the B-stairwell.

Instinct—and training—directed her to the stairwell. Her destination as building manager for One World Trade Center was the Fire Command Desk located in the northwest corner of the main lobby. This was her designated spot from which she would serve as the civilian incident commander, communicating with her staff, coworkers, World Trade Center tenants, and police and fire personnel.

Jerry Dinkels went over to the elevator with the ringing alarm and pried the door open a couple of inches. The cab was one floor below on the seventy-first floor.

"Help! Help!" people yelled from inside, trapped in the elevator cab. "Help! Get us out! The smoke!"

"Try to stay calm," Jerry shouted down to them through the top of the elevator cab. "I'll be right back with help," he said, leaving, the doors closing.

Going to the C-stairwell, Jerry saw a bunch of people from the engineering department who hadn't yet started down: Frank Lombardi, Achille Niro, Jack Spencer, Tim Volanakis, Mark Jakubek, and Peter Zipf.

"Guys," Jerry addressed the group, "people are trapped in the elevator."

"Okay—" Before Jerry could tell them the cab was on the floor below, they all ran over to the elevator. When they realized that it was on the seventy-first floor, they all turned back and ran down the stairs. The seventy-first-floor doors were unlocked and allowed access to the floor. Running over to the elevator they pried open the doors, but couldn't get them open beyond a few inches. There were two people trapped, and Jerry and the others knew them: Rob Eisenstat, a principal architect, and Frank Buckler, an electrical job shopper.

"Hey, guys!" Everybody started talking at once, reassuring them. "We're going to get you out of there." They were calm. And the smoke seemed to have abated.

Eight sets of hands, four per door, all pulled. They braced their feet on the doorframe, grunting, trying to pull the doors open.

Nothing! No movement. Net gain: zero.

They all tried again, redoubling their efforts, bodies getting in the way of bodies, mumbling, perspiring, yelling.

Score: Elevator, two. Rescuers, zero.

"Let's get some tools," someone suggested. The engineering department had an architectural model shop on the seventy-third floor. As everybody ran up to the model shop, Jerry stayed behind to keep the two trapped colleagues company.

"Where is everyone?" Jerry asked, looking around the empty space, wondering why it was so quiet, and empty.

"Go," a stranger instructed walking by. "The firemen will be here soon."

"Nah," Jerry replied. "I'm gonna wait."

"Don't worry, guys," Jerry said reassuringly, turning to speak between the few inches of open space in the elevator doors, "I'll wait with you."

The stairwell door banged open and the whole gang—*the cavalry*, he thought—came back from the model shop holding a thin piece of metal. To Jerry it first looked like an iron bar. Then he realized that it was a big, heavy-duty stapler used in the making of models.

They tried every which way to make that metal stapler open the door. Time and time again, they had no success.

Rob Eisenstat, one of the trapped victims, called out from between the doors, "Why don't you see if we can get some clippers so I can cut the cable?"

"You can't cut the cable, Rob—" Jerry stated.

"No!" Rob interrupted, "the door cable!"

Upstairs ran the cavalry again, and Jerry stayed back so the two men wouldn't be alone, fearing they were being abandoned.

Medhi walked by and said, "Jerry, go."

"No, Medhi. You go. I'll stay."

"No, Jerry. You go. I'll stay."

"Medhi?" Jerry asked quietly, "Do you have young children?"

"Yes, I do."

"Mine are grown," Jerry stated with understanding. "You go."

"Thank you, Jerry," Medhi said with deep gratitude as he turned and disappeared into the A-stairwell on the east side of the tower.

The cavalry banged through the stairwell door again, a pair of clippers clasped victoriously in their hands, and passed them through the door to Rob.

Rob reached up into the workings of the door and cut the cable.

The doors slid wide open.

"Let's get the hell out of here!" the cavalry chorused.

Officer David Lim looked up the east face of Tower One. What he saw shocked him. There were flames and smoke high in the tower. He was too close to the building to make an accurate guesstimate, but he knew it was way up there. Debris was still falling. It was raining fire—and another body was tumbling down.

David sprinted back into the "safety" of the mezzanine, brushing past the ever-increasing numbers of evacuees and began climbing up the A-stairwell. People made way for him, moving to the handrail as he continued to climb, his right shoulder to the outside wall. All the way up, David encouraged calmness and steadiness to those going down. When he reached the twenty-seventh floor, there was a man in a motorized wheelchair partly through the doorway, partly on the stairs. David stopped to assist. A moment later the men of the Fire Department of the City of New York, the FDNY, in complete bunker gear, came gasping and wheezing onto the floor from a separate stairway. They were already exhausted and had to take a brief breather. David took a break with them and told them about the man in the wheelchair. They stated that they would take care of him and carry him down, and that David should continue with what he was doing.

After breaking into a locked office to get some fresh air, David grabbed a telephone to call his wife, Diane.

"Hi, Diane, it's me," he said, after she answered on the first ring. "I'm all right. I'm going higher in the tower to find more people to get out."

"I've been watching television, and it looks pretty serious. Real bad," she replied.

"I'll be safe, dear. This is what we're trained to do," he said reassuringly, trying to keep her calm. "I've got to go. Give Debra and Michael a hug for me."

"Be careful. I love you." It was not easy being the wife of a police officer. "Okay."

The morning was young. A foreboding atmosphere hung heavy, as an invisible blanket of aviation gasoline began tightening its wrap within the tower . . .

###

8:53 A.M.

Erik Ronningen exited the men's room and found the core deserted. Whitney Birch was nowhere to be seen. As he passed by the east A and B stairwells looking for Whitney, he noticed that the carpets were soaked. When he reached the main freight elevator, it sounded like Victoria Falls behind the doors, and he watched as water poured from between them. Erik felt an impending doom in the air. The seventy-first floor was vacant and silent, and slowly filling with smoke. He opened the C-stairwell door and looked for Whitney, but she was nowhere to be seen amongst the employees streaming down the stairs. *Perhaps she went to the ladies room*, he reasoned. Erik closed the door and crossed back to the east side of the core and knocked loudly, calling her name. "Whitney! Whitney, are you in there?" Nothing. It was silent, except for the sound of water coursing down the freight elevator shaft.

On a windy day the movement of the tower could be heard as it softly groaned, gently swaying from side-to-side, performing as its architects and engineers had designed, and contractors had built it. But this morning there was no wind. Through the increasing haze of smoke, Erik could hear a cracking sound, a snapping from within the structure, and an occasional grinding. Walking away from the ladies room, he sloshed through the increasingly soaked carpet and glanced apprehensively at the freight elevator door discharging water. He returned to the southwest C-stairwell and opened the door. He had lost Whitney. Now his intent was to go to the upper levels to provide whatever help he could. *Surely they need some help up there*, he thought. But there was a flood of humanity pouring down the narrow stairwell from the upper floors. There was no way he could fight his way up, past the downward flow of evacuees. There was only one remaining course of action, and that was to join the flow downward.

###

From time to time in years past, Erik would walk the stairs from his office, then on the thirty-fifth floor of Tower Two, up to the forty-third-floor cafeteria of Morgan Stanley Dean Witter. The experience always left him breathing a little harder than he liked, and it took a day or so for his legs to return to normal. And that was only eight floors . . .

Anticipating the seventy-one-floor, 142-flight descent, Erik said a quick prayer to his Lord and Master—*Please assist my body to have sufficient strength to safely negotiate all these stairs*—and then stepped in and joined the multitudes in the downward exodus. After a few revolutions he spotted Whitney and, with a little effort, squeezed past people and caught up with her.

"How are you doing?" he asked.

"I'm okay, Erik. It's awful smoky in here. Do you have a handkerchief I could use to cover my nose and mouth?" she asked.

"Sure, here," he responded, handing her a second handkerchief he always carried in his left jacket pocket. "It's clean," he added as an afterthought, anticipating the question going through her mind.

"Thanks."

At the sixty-ninth-floor landing, Erik saw a familiar face. "Hello, John," he said to John Abruzzo, who was sitting in his wheelchair surrounded by a group of men. "Are you okay? Do you need any help?" he offered.

"We're fine," one of the men replied. "We're getting the emergency chair for John. We're all going to help get him down," he confirmed.

"Okay, John. Keep the faith. See you later," Erik encouraged, and continued his journey down with Whitney.

After ten or so minutes of descending, round and round uncounted times, a woman wearing a Sony Walkman announced, "Another plane has hit the building!" This declaration received less than the anticipated reaction. Everyone seemed to know that a plane had hit the tower, and an announcement from a woman listening to the radio only confirmed that the press was capitalizing on the occasion.

The circular parade continued, one floor number blurring into the next.

"Next week," Whitney said softly, her voice muffled through the handkerchief and her hand, "let's get together for a beer."

"Deal," Erik replied.

Helena Marietta was a country girl from Montana. She'd had her share of difficulty growing up helping her Daddy on his horse ranch. She'd been caught in a stampede or two, and had been taught the value of staying calm and using your head. These lessons had many benefits now in the elevator.

"Listen up, everybody," she shouted, getting their attention. "We're in trouble here." It was the understatement of her life. "It's hard to breathe, hot as hell, and I want everyone to stop talking, and to calm down," she said in her husky western accent. "We don't know how long this elevator will hold, so you big guys, there," she instructed, pointing to a couple of large men, "work at getting those elevator doors open. Let's see if we can start by getting a little air in here."

Yvonne Barker and Flory looked into the black void. Inhaling smoke, they slammed the door shut, trapped. Turning to look at each other, they both ran back into their office space, careful to avoid the hole in the floor.

"Call somebody!" Yvonne said. Flory responded, "I'm going to call my wife."

"Okay," was all Yvonne said. She was trying to think whom she could call. In February of 1993, when the World Trade Center was bombed, she had called her best friend, but he wasn't there. So nobody had known what she was going through. She wanted to actually talk to someone this time to let them know.

While she was thinking, she kicked off her high heels and crawled under her desk, looking for her sneakers. No sneakers. Amidst the debris, however, she did find a pair of flats, so she put them on. Yvonne also pulled out her backpack, which was caught between the legs of the desk and the wall, and dumped the contents of her pocketbook, and any other ready items she thought she might need, into it.

Then she dialed her sister-in-law's telephone number.

"Hello?" her friend and sister-in-law answered.

"I don't know what's happened!" Yvonne blurted, crying hysterically. "Please call my daughter and tell her I love her. I don't think I'm getting out!" Then she hung up.

When she looked up, she saw Flory standing there, ready to try again to get out, when her phone rang. Bewildered, she answered it. It was a girlfriend of hers from Maryland.

"Something has happened," she informed Yvonne. "I just heard that something has happened."

Crying, Yvonne bawled into the phone, "I gotta go! I gotta go!" And she hung up.

Immediately her phone rang again. Yvonne was frantic. She picked it up and yelled, "I have to go! I have to go!"

It was her ex-husband's wife, her daughter's stepmother. "Something's happened," she yelled into the telephone. "Get out! Get out!"

"I'm getting out now!" Yvonne yelled, and threw the phone down.

8:56 A.M.

Nancy Seliga suffered from claustrophobia. She was not looking forward to another forced trip down the stairs. February 26, 1993, had involved enough stairs for a lifetime. But—here she was, making another descent down the B-stairwell, this time from the twenty-first floor.

Nancy was amazed at how calm most of the people were. Their calmness certainly had a calming effect on her, even though she continued to talk to herself in her head. She hated the closed-in feeling of the stairwell, even though it was brightly lit, and all these people packed into so confined a space. And just like with the 1993 bombing, there was a little smoke in the stairwell again this morning. Not a good sign . . .

She was having real trouble breathing, either from the claustrophobia or from the smoke—or both. So she, Bob Benacchio, and Bern D'Leo left the stairwell and went into the office spaces on the thirteenth floor. As she caught her breath, the other two walked around the floor to make certain no one had remained behind. The floor was empty.

"Are you all right, Nancy?" Bob asked. "Would you like to just wait here?"

"No," she replied. "Something's wrong. Let's just go."

As she continued her descent, a man near her yelled, "It's a bomb!"

"No, sir, it's not," Nancy said to him reassuringly. "Please just continue walking calmly down the stairs." Summoning her strength of will, she was the very picture of unruffled composure. "Everything will be okay," she said comfortingly.

There was the normal speculation and understandable panic just under the surface of the uninitiated. But as building manager for the tower, Nancy was well known to most, if not all, the tenant employees, and as they nervously asked her what had happened, she calmed them as best she could.

In spite of all that was developing, Nancy couldn't help but feel a "pride of ownership." She was in charge of the life safety of the employees in her tower. And thanks to sufficient, proper training, the employees immediately took it upon themselves to evacuate, without waiting for "professionally trained" guidance. More than once, the presidents of the more prestigious firms had reminded her that it cost them "X-bucks every time we are required to accommodate one of your drills!" Nancy had never thought she required vindication, but today she had it. *You can't make this stuff up!* she thought, repeating one of Doug Karpiloff's favorite expressions.

After more turns going down the stairs, a woman's voice screamed out, "I can't handle this anymore!" Someone was carrying a portable radio, and the announcer had just reported that another plane had hit the towers.

"No, no, no . . ." Nancy said soothingly, placing her hand on the woman's arm. "Let's just keep walking down. We're almost there."

She shouldered her way through a few folks. "Excuse me. Pardon," she said apologetically, reaching the person with the radio. "Sir, can you please turn that off for now? Thank you."

8:58 A.M.

Briefcase in hand, heading for the exit, Tad heard his telephone begin to ring. Turning back, he reached for it, picked up the receiver, and said, "Hello?"

"What the hell are you still doing up there?" a familiar voice shouted. It was his brother calling from Poland. "You'd better get your ass downstairs because from what I hear, it is a serious situation!"

"Okay, brother. I'm doing it."

Walking once again toward the exit, briefcase firmly gripped in his hand, Tad had to pass their little kitchen. Remembering that he had purchased some fruit at the Liberty Street open-air market the day before, he made a side trip and pitched a couple of apples, a drink, and a container of yogurt into his case. *Reinforcements for the road,* he thought.

Tad, another engineer named Sam Sharma, and a consultant named Nick Scinicariello hurried up to the north door, one of four leading out into the elevator lobby. Pushing the door it immediately jammed, opening only enough to poke one's head through.

"What the hell?" Tad said to his associates. "It's black in there. The walls are fallen in and there is debris all over the place. We've got to find another way out," he instructed. "This is more serious than I thought." The realization of their predicament began to dawn on him.

###

8:59 A.M.

Two flaming bodies had just run silently past Captain Anthony Whitaker in the dark mall. He made a quick assessment of the situation. He got on his radio and called the World Trade Center Police Command Desk located on the mezzanine level of Building Five.

"This is Captain Whitaker. I want to start an immediate building evacuation of Towers One and Two, and the whole World Trade Center complex."

Tony didn't know the cause of this catastrophe, but whatever the cause he knew he had to take immediate action. In his thirty years of law enforcement, he had received no training that could convince him that there was any other right course of action than to get all the people out of all the buildings—immediately. Tony knew the situation was bad and beyond his ability as commanding officer to do anything about. He felt that it only seemed prudent to start a full-scale evacuation of the entire complex and get everyone out.

He then got in touch with Sergeant Marty Duane, one of his sergeants who was attached to the PATH Command, and gave orders to assign Port Authority cops at strategic locations throughout the mall to direct and facilitate the evacuation.

9:01 A.M.

Gabriella Ballini watched as Myron Finegold stood up on a desk in the inspector general's office on the seventy-sixth floor to get everyone's attention, announcing that he knew a way out of the tower and that everyone should follow him.

Greg Reszka looked for an exit sign and led his little group out into the corridor, past what looked like a blown-out electrical closet that was on fire. Gabriella saw a man in a suit handling a fire hose, attempting to put out a fire as their little group clambered over the blown-out rubble walls, and entered another stairwell going down.

This stairwell was crowded with people, too, but it was very orderly, Gabriella observed. She bumped into some colleagues, and as they speculated on the morning's bizarre turn of events, Gabriella now became aware of smoke in this stairwell and water on the stairs—and the humidity and heat. It was so hot!

And down and down they continued until they reached the floors in the sixties, when the whole progression began to bottleneck.

"Take something for your face," Flory advised Yvonne Barker. He, too, had been in the bombing nearly nine years ago, and remembered as if it were yesterday the long, three-hour smoky climb down and out. "Take something for your face—like that," he said, pointing to a couple of T-shirts on a file cabinet.

A client had recently given them T-shirts as a thank you, so Yvonne grabbed two, took them to the water fountain on the way out, and soaked them both.

Carefully crawling through their previously made exit next to the hole in the floor, they went through the outer offices on the eighty-sixth floor. Yvonne was struck by the fact that they were the only two people on the entire one-acre floor. *Where is everyone?* she thought.

As she wrapped the wet T-shirt around her nose and mouth, Flory opened the door into the tower core. It was total blackness and smoke. But countless fire drills had trained them to go directly to the C-stairwell. They knew exactly where it was, even in the dark. In fact, she remembered that in 1993 it was the same one she used to get out.

When she opened the door, it was clear where everyone was; they were in the stairwells, evacuating! She could barely squeeze into the crowd.

Tad Hanc and his colleagues tried a second of four doors that led into the tower core—only to be confronted with more blackness and debris. Not wishing to climb over all that wreckage in the darkness, Tad Hanc—the image of the airliner flying directly toward him permanently burned into his memory—with his colleagues Sam Sharma and Nick Scinicariello, went for the third door. This route was sufficiently clear of wreckage. "We'll go down the A-stairwell," Tad said matter-of-factly, and they began their eighty-six-floor hike down and out of Tower One.

After confirming that all his office staff members had evacuated the basement offices, Jim Usher made his way up to the concourse level of Tower Two. Taking the escalator two steps at a time, he strode purposefully toward the double doors that opened to the plaza. None of Jim's training or experience could have prepared him for what confronted him there.

It was a disaster zone. The plaza was full of debris, glass, metal . . . and paper. It looked like hundreds of tons of paper falling out of the sky, burning. Jim was dumbfounded by the sight, and stood transfixed for several moments when he realized that there were several injured people standing in the plaza not that far away from him. Without a moment's hesitation, or a second thought for his own safety, Jim pushed through the doors and went to the aid of the nearest man.

"Put your left arm around my neck and shoulders," he instructed the confused, bleeding man. "I'll help get you to the infirmary. You'll be all right," he added, trying to comfort the man. Another person was standing nearby, and Jim told him that he would be right back to help him, too.

Jim had returned to the plaza and was about twenty feet from the base of Tower Two when the heavens directly above exploded and disintegrated into total chaos.

9:03 A.M.

We've got a problem here. Vic Guarnera's radio crackled again with information that a plane had crashed into Tower Two. *Those bozos,* Vic thought with frustration. *They don't know what they're talking about! How can they confuse Tower One with Tower Two?*

"S5, SCC." It was Jonesie from the Security Command Center on the twenty-second floor of Tower One calling Vic on the radio.

"SCC, S5, Jonesie, are you okay?"

"Vic," Jonesie blurted, "we can't get out! The sally-port door is jammed!"

"Okay, Jonesie," Vic responded. "Stay calm. I'm on my way."

Vic walked down the escalator with the flow of traffic and continued to direct the evacuees out of the North Tower toward West Street. Ernesto Butcher, chief operations officer for the Port Authority, was at the B-corridor turnstiles conversing with some of the senior staff. Ernesto acknowledged Vic's nod of hello as he passed heading to the B-stairwell.

"SCC, S5," Vic said into his radio transmitting to Jonesie, "I'm leaving the main lobby and am on my way up now. I'll be there in a few minutes," he announced rather optimistically. For his sixty-seven years, Vic was in pretty good shape. He didn't stop more than once or twice to catch his breath during his ascent to the twenty-second floor. On his climb up he met a number of associates walking down.

"Hey, Vic!" someone called. "You're going the wrong way. You have to go *down* to leave the tower," they half joked.

"I have people trapped in the SCC," Vic responded. "I'm going up to get them out."

He saw Mo Lipson, an eighty-nine-year-old gentleman who had retired from the Port Authority in 1982. *Oh, thank God he's getting out,* Vic thought. Then he saw Tina Hansen, a friend and beautiful young woman, being carried down in her lightweight motorized wheelchair.

"Ah, the queen being carried down in her throne by two handsome, able-bodied royal coachmen," Vic chided Tina.

The fear was visible in her eyes as she gave him a little of her beautiful smile.

"Stay well, Tina," Vic encouraged. "I'll see you later." And Vic continued climbing up to the twenty-second floor.

###

Jim Usher half walked, half jogged to an injured person standing near the base of the east side of the South Tower. He had returned to the plaza after delivering another injured man to the infirmary. He never made it to the standing man.

The entire world above Jim exploded. The shock wave threw him to the ground; his ears heard an eruption of thunder never before experienced, and he went instantly deaf. The flash of heat was as if he were the Thanksgiving turkey ten minutes shy of being removed from the oven. He craned his neck and head around his prostrate body, looked up, and the sight froze in his memory. In that split instant in time, Jim saw the tower disintegrate into a million pieces of metal and large orange fireballs as big around as the five-acre plaza. And gravity pulled the entire confused molten mass of tortuous heat and destruction down, directly upon him.

Jim had never given much thought to religion, and he certainly never thought about death—his death. He thought of it now, and knew with certainty that he was going to die. Thinking of his two daughters, and remembering that he had a digital camera in his jacket pocket, he quickly pulled it out and in one fluid motion pointed it straight up at the tsunami of splintered glass, cascading javelins of steel, smoke, and fireballs—and snapped his final photograph. When they pulled his dead, mutilated body out of the wreckage, he reasoned, and found the camera firmly clutched in his right hand, he wanted his daughters to know the cause of his death.

###

Officer David Lim had made it to the forty-fourth-floor sky lobby in Tower One. This was a transfer lobby from the twelve express elevators in the main lobby to the twenty-four local elevators going to tenant offices between the forty-fifth and seventy-fifth floors.

David was helping to direct the ever-increasing flow of evacuees away from the nonworking express elevators and into the stairwells. He was near the east windows when he turned for a moment, looking out, and saw a tremendous explosion coming from the north and east sides of the South Tower, up near the eightieth floors, he guessed. The fireballs kept exploding, the noise unimaginable. One fireball came straight down to his window, and as he turned to run—there was no thought or emotion, only reflexes—it exploded.

The world went into slow motion. David tumbled through the air, chunks of plate glass hurtling past him. A couple of firemen and a few civilians flew through the air alongside him. They crash-landed, arms and legs flailing against one another. The clothing on a few civilians was burning, but others came to their aid and quickly extinguished the flames.

The scene was both one of pandemonium and absolute cooperation. Many of the uninjured had panicked and were running, screaming toward any of the three stairwells, trying to cram themselves into the stream of evacuees walking down from higher in the tower. The injured were immediately assisted by others who had unselfishly come to their aid, smothering the clothing fires, tending to the burned, picking up the fallen, and supporting the injured, escorting them down the stairs.

Training, and human compassion toward one's fellow man, is a beautiful thing, David Lim realized.

Picking himself up, he discovered that he was neither burnt nor injured. *A miracle*, he thought, and immediately continued with his duties helping people out of the sky lobby and into the stairs going down.

In a moment of reflection, Officer Lim was thankful for the excellent training he had received from his old training sergeants. Those sergeants were excellent instructors; were it not for their thoroughness in teaching how to conduct oneself in emergency situations, he would not now be as valuable an asset.

Captain Anthony Whitaker was checking out the area around Saint Nicholas Greek Orthodox Church when he heard an earsplitting roar and a huge sucking sound. That little voice in the back of his head said *don't look up*. And Tony obeyed. In the same instant, there was a stupendous explosion, and a millisecond later, he saw an enormous fireball crashing out of the other side of the tower with the accompanying heat wave punching him in the side of the face. He was near a door and it flew open as he flung himself inside, escaping the probable burns and injuries from falling debris.

"What's happening? What's going on?" the crowd of trapped people were asking him. Tony was a big man in the uniform of a police captain, and people naturally turned to him for instructions.

"Stay calm and don't panic," Tony instructed them. "We're doing everything possible to bring the situation under control." Just before he exited the building, he further instructed, "Don't go outdoors. As long as you're in the church you will be safe." And he stepped out of God's sanctuary into the Devil's living nightmare.

###

9:04 A.M.

"All units. Request a ranking police officer report to the Fire Command Desk in the North Tower." This came from the World Trade Center Police Command Desk.

"This is Whitaker," the captain said into his radio. "I'll respond."

When Tony got to the Command Desk, he was surprised to see three close friends, all senior police officers who had come down from the Holland Tunnel. *How'd they get down here so fast?* Tony wondered. He also saw John O'Neill, recently retired from the FBI and hired by Larry Silverstein. He was with Doug Karpiloff and others from the Mayor's Office of Emergency Management. As Tony began to look around, he was shocked to notice many of the windows blown out and firemen knocking out the rest with their axes. That was when he began hearing the sickening thud, very much like the sound of a shotgun going off, of falling bodies from the upper floors crashing onto the overhead covering of VIP Drive.

Captain Whitaker received orders to set up a command center in the South Tower. He took his three longtime friends with him, and as he walked past the express elevators to the seventy-eighth floor, he noticed they were not operational.

###

9:05 A.M.

Jim Usher's body was one of many so carelessly strewn about the plaza. When he came to, he just lay there not knowing his condition—or whereabouts. As the fog began to lift from his brain, his first realization was that every inch of his body was in prickly pain. His hearing had returned and he heard the hissing of objects hurtling down all around him, and the *thunk* sound of the objects as they imbedded in the plaza terrazzo. When he opened his eyes, in a flash he was back in the bug-infested fields of Cambodia. Except this wasn't razor grass. It was acres of shredded glass and mutilated steel impaled all around him. Miraculously, the twisted javelins of metal had missed his body, but he felt like how the pretty lady must have felt standing at the receiving end of the knife-throwing act in the carnival he went to as a kid.

Jim performed a quick mental inventory of all his parts. Except for the prickly pain all over, and blood oozing out of his skin everywhere, he seemed okay. Determining that his present location was not safe, he rolled onto all fours, carefully stood, testing his balance, and as quickly as he could, navigated through the debris field, down the steps to Liberty Street, and out of the immediate area to safety.

###

9:06 A.M.

Unlike the evacuation in 1993, when the stairwells were pitch black, Yvonne Barker observed that the stairwells were brightly lit. And this time you could see the thick, the very thick, smoke. Yvonne knew that it was much, much worse this time. She hadn't seen any injuries in '93, but this morning, she had seen people with torn clothing and people helping others with blood all over them, and some looked like they had been terribly burned.

Down and down she went with all the others. The people were very calm, she noted, in spite of all the smoke. *Thank God Flory thought of these T-shirts*, she thought, readjusting hers to a fresher, wetter section.

The stairs must be blocked, Yvonne concluded, because everyone was leaving through one of the floors in the seventies.

"Be careful of this hole in the floor," a man in a business suit wielding a fire hose was telling people as they walked past. He was fighting a fire all by himself!

Yvonne was amazed. She would have liked to have helped, but she was so scared for herself and everyone else, that all she could do was say a little prayer for him and keep up with the crowd.

Flory continued to remain by Yvonne's side as they entered another stairwell going down. When they got to the sixty-eighth floor, she saw Tina Hansen. Some men were transferring her from her motorized wheelchair to an evac-u-chair, a lightweight evacuation chair stored in the stairwells of each floor. They were preparing to carry her by hand down the stairs.

"Are you okay, Tina?" Yvonne heard Flory ask.

The look on Tina's face was one of total fear. She'd been through this before too, all too soon ago. And now memory was bringing that past immediately into the present—as if it had happened only yesterday. Eight and a half years ago since last being evacuated in a similar manner suddenly seemed like only yesterday to Tina.

Tina could only nod her head up and down in acknowledgment of Flory's inquiry as she was manhandled into the evac-u-chair.

9:08 A.M.

The three colleagues hadn't been climbing down the stairs more than a few minutes when Tad Hanc noticed reddish water pouring down the stairs. "What is this?" he said to no one in particular. "Maybe some rust in the sprinkler water or something," he answered himself distractedly. As the reddish water increased in volume, and the stairs became increasingly slippery, Tad leaned down to roll up his trouser legs. It was an awkward procedure. He kept a firm right-hand grip on his briefcase, not wanting to place it in the running water, while rolling up his trousers with his left hand. That task accomplished, the three of them continued down.

"The door is locked," Tad Hanc stated matter-of-factly. "Or stuck." They had arrived at the crossover at the seventy-sixth floor. The crossover was a detour, a small passageway in the stairwell that went around heavy mechanical equipment installed in the tower, before the stairs continued down. "The door won't budge," he said calmly as he began kicking it, hoping to jar it open. Tad was not a small man, and one of the others, larger than Tad, added his weight to the task of forcing the door open. But to no avail. The door would not budge. Though he was a civil engineer, it didn't occur to Tad at the time that the violently swaying tower had wedged the door tightly in its frame.

Calmly, and without discussion, the three arrived at the same conclusion, turned around, and began to climb back up. The stairs were slippery with the reddish water, which had increased and was now leaking off the ceilings above them. Gripping the handrails with their free hands, they worked their way back up to the eighty-sixth floor.

9:10 A.M.

Captain Anthony Whitaker and the three other police officers from the Holland Tunnel walked through the dark mall to the South Tower to establish a command center and set up telephone lines to the various police commands throughout the Trade Center.

"Captain," said a fire chief to Tony, "I need an escort for my men and myself into the tower."

"Nat," Tony said, turning to his old friend Nathaniel Webb, "go with the chief." Tony could see that Nat was reluctant to go up into the tower, but he was the only officer available for the escort, so he went.

After receiving another call on his tactical radio to go meet with the chief, Tony left the command center and headed to Liberty Street. As he was about to step outside, that voice in the back of his head spoke to him again, warning him not to go outdoors. So he waded through the mall and exited up near Vesey and Church Streets. When he got outdoors, he looked up. And for the first time, he saw the magnitude of the disaster: both Towers were lit up, on fire, and there was total panic. It was a scene from hell. Total chaos reigned. A few minutes later Tony ran into the new manager for the World Trade Center, Geoffrey Wharton.

"I've got to get back into the tower to check on my colleagues on the eighty-eighth floor," Geoffrey announced to Tony.

"You can't go back in there," Tony told him. "It's too dangerous." After instructing Geoffrey to evacuate the area, Tony walked through the devastation of Vesey Street to West Street and situated himself under the North Bridge connecting the World Trade Center to the World Financial Center.

Startled by the sounds of explosions, Tony realized it was the sounds of falling bodies crashing onto the pavement. There was also a continuous rain of debris. Noticing a police emergency vehicle, he instructed the officer to move the vehicle closer to the World Financial Center, where it would be safe.

As Tony began walking down West Street to get a better assessment of the situation, he saw a woman walking toward him. She was in her mid-forties or early fifties. It was impossible to tell because, to Tony's horror, her clothes had burned completely off. Her skin was blackened and still smoking. She was in a daze; when Tony stepped toward her to assist, two firemen intercepted, moved her to the curb, and took charge.

At last, Nancy Seliga thought, relieved, reaching the door leading into the main lobby. Pushing through after the person in front of her, she stepped three paces into the B-corridor before her brain registered the sight around her. Her mind froze, as did her body, coming to an abrupt stop. She thought her eyes were betraying her. "This is a war zone," she murmured to herself. Nancy immediately knew this was a much worse situation than the bombing in February 1993. She was there then, and this did not even compare. "A war zone," she repeated.

Turning her head, she saw Ernie Anemone standing next to her, and she asked, "What happened?"

Ernie's eyes filled with tears. His mouth was moving but there was no sound.

"Ernie," she implored, "did a plane hit the building?"

His answer immediately confirmed her intuition from earlier. "Yeah," he said with factual resignation.

"What floor?" she asked. Normally, Nancy would have known all the answers moments after the event. As building manager she carried a radio and was connected to all World Trade Center management staff, but the traffic was so heavy she couldn't get through to anyone.

"I don't know," he admitted.

"But, aren't Alan and all the others up there?" she asked. Her question betrayed the fear that was gnawing at the edge of her disciplined self-control. She was referring to Alan Reiss, director of the World Trade Department, and all her coworkers still located on the eighty-eighth floor.

"I don't know," was all that Ernie answered.

Nancy just stood there, looking around, not believing what her eyes were registering. Elevators six and seven were hanging out of their shafts, doors blown out. The marble was hanging off the walls and in piles on the floor. She and Ernie began to walk, scuffling through debris that was littering her immaculate corridor, to the turnstiles exiting toward the mall. Looking, but not believing what she was seeing, her goal was the Fire Command Desk.

9:16 A.M.

Nancy Seliga, in a daze, walked with Ernie Anemone to the turn-stiles. Ernesto Butcher, chief operating officer of the Port Authority, was on the other side when they arrived.

"Nancy, it's going to be okay," Ernesto said, seeing her state of mind written on her face.

"I just have to get over to the Fire Desk."

"No," Ernesto said, "you've got to get out."

"No, I can't. I've got to get over to the Fire Command Desk," she repeated.

"Nance!" he responded firmly, using the nickname only her closest Port Authority friends could call her, emphasizing the urgency of the situation. "Go to the hotel and just get out of the tower!"

"I can't." Nancy knew where she was supposed to report. She was in charge of the tower, her tower, and she had a responsibility to fulfill to her tenants and their employees. She had work to do.

"Ernie," Ernesto said, turning to him. "Just get her out of here," he commanded.

Jerry Dinkels and company, the cavalry, having successfully rescued the people trapped in the elevator, filed into the A-stairwell on the east side of the seventy-first-floor core and began their descent. The stairwell was fairly clear of smoke and people. Since they descended at different paces, the valiant rescue team soon became separated.

In the course of Jerry's journey down the stairs, he ran into some of the people from the Port Authority Controller's Department. A couple of them were carrying a gurney with a burn victim. As he approached the forty-fourth-floor sky lobby, Jerry began to see pockets of firemen. *They're so young*, Jerry noticed, realizing the older ones—who were slower—were certainly not far behind.

###

9:20 A.M.

The floor placards blurred: *68 . . . 62 . . . 57 . . . 51 . . .*

"Is that you, John?" Erik Ronningen shouted down to John Moriarty from the comptroller's office. John had just looked up from a flight below, and Erik just happened to be looking down.

"Yep, Erik. It's me," he replied. "I sure hate having to walk down all these stairs," he commented.

"I'm happy to be able to do so," Erik countered.

"I hear you!"

Erik saw the friendly face of Mary Jones, a longtime Port Authority employee who worked in the mail room, who was resting at a floor stairwell platform. "Hello, Mary," Erik said, placing his hand on her shoulder. She looked tired, and the gesture was intended to calm and encourage. "How are you doing?" he asked quietly.

"I'm just taking a little rest before I continue," she said in her soft voice. "These steps aren't as easy as they were in '93," she joked.

"You can make it," Erik said confidently. "Don't despair."

46 . . . 39 . . . 32 . . . Round and round, flight after flight, the relentless shuffle of thousands of feet scuffled on the stair treads. The end seemed an eternity away. In the semi-quiet of the descent, Erik could faintly hear the snapping of pipes, an unmistakable sound, like ice cracking on a pond on a cold winter's day. No one was aware of it, but the tower was in the beginning of its death throes.

"Step aside!" someone yelled. "Coming up!" New York City firemen were walking up, struggling against the tide. Erik could see the exhaustion from carrying all their equipment to fight the fires in the upper tower.

All of the stairwell lights were on, and Erik was aware how calm everyone was, in spite of the thickening smoke. No panic. No outward impatience. There was just continued, controlled progress downward. *27 . . . 22 . . .* He had not realized that he had just passed the Backup Security Command Center located on the twenty-second floor of Tower One. His only goal now was to get to the Operations Command Center located in the safety of the basement levels of Tower Two, the South Tower, to help his best friend, Doug Karpiloff, director of security and life safety for the World Trade Center.

Round and round they all continued down . . .

Liz Kelly, Sarah Ronningen's best friend, telephoned her at the office a second time and offered, "If you decide to go home, why don't you come spend the day with Jackie and me?"

Why would I want to go home? Sarah thought. The hair began to stand up on the back of her neck, and now she was becoming a little more concerned by Liz's concern for her welfare. *What is going on?* she silently asked herself.

"Okay. Thanks, Liz," she replied. "I'll call you back in a little while." Sarah hung up and continued with the paperwork documenting that the new realtors had taken their required indoctrination class.

Tad Hanc and his two companions climbed back to the eighty-sixth floor, exited the stairwell, and entered another of the three stairwells going down. This one was full of people calmly evacuating from the upper tower. Tad's mind flashed back to the World Trade Center bombing of February 1993. He observed that unlike all the smoky and darkened stairwells back then, today there was no smoke, though it was pretty hot, and the stairwells were brightly lit. *Everything is working perfectly*, he thought.

"Is that you, Frank?" Tad asked a colleague who was supposed to meet with him in the basement B-6 level for the inspection. "Well, I don't think we'll be doing the inspection today," Tad joked. "Maybe we have to change the appointment for another day."

Tad became aware that he had become separated from his original two companions. There were a lot of people in the stairwell evacuating, and people stopped to let those helping the handicapped pass, which slowed the progress. As he looked, he spotted his friend Patricia Cullen—"Trish" to her friends—who was a property manager for the Port Authority. He accompanied Trish down, and at each floor, they tried to open the doors leading into the office spaces, seeing if there was anything they could do to help. When they got to around the seventy-first floor, Trish had to use the ladies room. Since everyone was calm in the stairwell, and there was no talk of immediate danger, Tad let her go, saying, "Okay, but I'm continuing down."

Nancy Seliga, some of her staff, and a few coworkers walked through the lobby of Tower One and entered directly into the Marriott Hotel. As they attempted to set up a command center, Nancy turned to one of Larry Silverstein's staff and asked, "Have you talked to anyone on eighty-eight?"

"I couldn't reach anyone up there," he replied.

Nancy tried calling on her radio: "94," her call signal, "to 56," Alan Reiss's. No reply. The radio traffic was beyond jammed.

"What are you doing?" a man's panicky voice screamed.

Nancy quickly turned to the screaming voice and saw that it belonged to a New York City police officer. "I'm Nancy Seliga, building manager of Tower One, and we're setting up our command center," she informed him as politely as she could, trying to calm him down.

"You have to get out, now!"

She started to protest, but then he yelled, "Get the *hell* out of the hotel!"

The panic in the officer's face, his explosive voice, and his expressive use of language was enough.

Nancy knew she'd better do as this guy said. The adrenaline began coursing through her veins as her heart rate doubled. The fear was contagious, and they all began running toward the Tall Ships bar in the hotel, which had the closest exits opening onto Liberty Street.

Slamming through the open door of Tall Ships, Bern D'Leo yelled, "Nance, run as fast as you can! Don't look up! Don't look down! Run as fast as you can!"

"What happened?" she asked.

The tears were streaming down Bern's face, and he screamed again, "Run as fast as you can!"

She ran out onto Liberty Street, and right in front of her, lying in the middle of the street—was an airline seat!

"Oh, my God!"

Crossing Liberty Street, Nancy stopped to turn around. All the cops and a couple of people started screaming at her, "Run across West Street! Don't stop! Run as fast as you can!"

And she ran.

Reaching the southwest side of West Street, Nancy stopped, turned around—and looked up. All along she had thought it was an accident and that only the North Tower had been struck. Now she knew—the South Tower had been hit while she was coming down the stairwell. In that moment all time in Nancy's world stood still.

Helena Marietta's calm, persistent encouragement and definitive instructions had their desired effect. The men got the elevator doors open. But the floor was a long way down, and the open shaft made it too dangerous to try to jump out and down. All they needed was to add a broken leg to their already impossible dilemma, or for someone to stumble into the open shaft. The upper floor was about seven feet up, and the choice was obvious.

"Okay, guys," Helena said, "get on your hands and knees and make a pyramid. Let's get the women out first." Helena was the last woman out and she found herself in some kind of equipment room. She went looking and found a couple of old chairs and stools, and pushed them into the elevator so the men could more easily climb out. After the last man got out, there were a couple of quick hugs, and then they all disappeared, working their own ways out of the tower.

9:24 A.M.

Once he assured himself that there was no one remaining in the forty-fourth-floor sky lobby, Officer David Lim and the few remaining firemen entered the B-stairwell going down. On the way they encountered several elderly requiring assistance, and a couple of physically handicapped. The firemen began dropping their equipment, picking up the handicapped, and carrying them down. David was doing everything possible to calm the elderly and to assist in the orderly evacuation.

The deteriorating conditions in the stairwell didn't contribute to David's calming efforts. There was some smoke, and dark, muddy water began cascading down the steps, making for slippery going. People had whatever material they could find covering their noses and mouths. Eyes stinging, faces covered, there wasn't much conversation, but David could see the fear in people's eyes. The progress down had slowed significantly.

"You're doing fine," he would encourage in his quiet, reassuring voice. "We're almost there. Just a few more floors and we're out."

9:26 A.M.

"Move aside! Move aside! Bloody people coming down," someone shouted from above them. Gabriella Ballini could see that the people coming down were bleeding through their torn clothing. She moved aside, as did the others, and then a man in a wheelchair was carried down by a group of other men.

As they descended, at one floor people were streaming into the stairwell. *They must have transferred from another stairwell,* Gabriella thought as she recognized many of her colleagues from the offices on the seventies. A woman walking next to her said that she had a cell phone. "Two airplanes, one hit each tower," she said.

"Terrorism!" Gabriella said right away. That was the only logical explanation. And then she got really worried again, as her mind went back to the structure of the tower, and the safety of the building. She thought back to what she felt about forty minutes ago . . . the tower shaking like an aftershock from an earthquake.

Dear God, Gabriella began her prayer again. *Dear God, please help me get out alive.* She so desperately wanted to get out and be with her husband and three children. She couldn't stop thinking about them most of the way down. Gabriella wasn't the only evacuee praying that morning.

She could see that plenty of other people were scared, and that they, too, were saying their own private prayers.

Gabriella noticed that they were only in the teen floors, and it had to have been nearly an hour since the plane crashed into the tower. The evacuation had come to a complete standstill.

9:30 A.M.

Jerry Dinkels left the stairwell and entered the forty-fourth-floor sky lobby. He was shocked as he slowly walked, looking side to side, across the lobby toward the other stairwell.

The lobby is trashed! he thought in dismay. Jerry saw broken glass, furniture overturned, scorched carpet and walls. The plateglass windows at the end of the lobby, on the east side, were broken out. Jerry couldn't fathom what had caused this kind of devastation. Walking, practically in a daze, Jerry entered a different stairwell and continued the long journey down.

A couple of flights down, Jerry noticed more firemen climbing up—all young, handsome, with all-American faces. And the look in their exhausted eyes was one of fear. They were very, very afraid, but they kept on climbing.

"Take care," some of the evacuating employees said, encouragingly. "Be careful up there."

Where did all this Gatorade, Snapple, and Poland Spring water come from? Jerry wondered. Suddenly, there was what seemed like hundreds of bottles being passed around. *Someone must have broken into something,* he thought, as they were being handed out. "Great idea," he said, taking a couple of bottles, keeping one for himself, and passing the others to some firemen who accepted them with much appreciation.

More firemen appeared and kept climbing, with an occasional chief in control. Jerry was in awe of the disciplined control of the men, climbing with all that heavy equipment, perspiring under the weight of their bunker gear, tired, exhausted. Yet they kept climbing.

May God bless, Jerry thought, saying a little prayer.

"Mo!" Jerry said, approaching Mo Lipson as he came down to a landing. "Mo, do you want me to carry you?" Jerry asked.

Jerry felt strong and thought he could carry Mo in a fireman's carry the remainder of the way down. Mo was a Port Authority institution. Retired at the age of seventy, he had been rehired as a consultant. He never quit working and was in great shape for an eighty-nine-year-old man.

"No, no," someone accompanying him responded. "He's okay," the person emphasized.

"All right," Jerry answered, turning on the landing and continuing down.

###

9:33 A.M.

Because there were so many people in the stairwell evacuating, the procession down grew very, very slow, and frequently everyone came to a standstill, not moving at all. After what seemed like an eternity, Tad Hanc saw some firemen passing them, climbing up into the tower.

The farther down the evacuees went, the hotter it got. *Boy, it's getting hot!* Tad thought. At this he took off his suit jacket and stuffed it into his briefcase. He then removed his white shirt and wrapped it around his waist and undershirt. Down, down he continued. Tad began to notice pieces of clothing, shoes, and handbags tossed aside on the stair landings, and lots and lots of coins. At one point, seeing a dime face up, he bent down and rescued it. *Just for good luck*, he thought. *Okay, this is going to save my life probably.* And down and down he continued with the never-ending procession.

###

9:36 A.M.

Yvonne Barker's body was exhausted. She had been climbing down, and climbing down through all this thick smoke, and she was as tired as everyone else looked. She considered herself fit for a grandmother, but she was a grandmother nevertheless, she acknowledged. Yvonne saw that they had descended into the twenties. Not only was the smoke thick, but there was also water everywhere, making the stairs especially slippery. *The sprinkler systems must have all turned on*, she thought.

"Stand aside, firemen coming up!" a chorus of voices announced. Yvonne noted how young they all looked. They had to be young. Look at all that heavy equipment they had to carry. And they were sweating.

"Do you want some water?" a couple of the ladies asked the firemen. "You want some water?" The women were handing out their bottles of water, and the firemen gratefully accepted them.

"Oh, I hope you did your exercises!" one woman joked. "Hope you're fit," another contributed, adding, "it's a long way up!" The firemen were laughing. Everyone was laughing, including Yvonne. She was grateful for the few moments of levity. She was exhausted, her nerves were shot, and she was scared. Like everyone else, she had but one goal: to get out of the towers.

9:41 A.M.

Nancy Seliga was in shock. Looking up from West Street, staring, she couldn't believe what was happening. Both towers were in flames! The smoke was billowing skyward, the blizzard of paper raining down. The streets were littered with paper, debris, and—*Jesus H.*—her mind locked, frozen. Did she just see what she thought she saw? *Her* tower . . . One World Trade Center . . . *bodies? People—jumping!?*

First things first; she wanted to telephone her husband, Chuck, who was driving to Boston for an early-morning meeting. Reaching for her cell phone, she remembered that she forgot to bring it with her when she gathered up all her stuff and left the office.

Nancy felt a hand on her shoulder. It was her close friend and coworker, Bob Benacchio. "Come on, Nance," he said gently, kindly. "Come on. Let's try to find a phone to call Chuck and my wife." They began walking south on West Street, and after several attempts elsewhere, at West Thames Street were able to use a phone at a Chinese dry-cleaning establishment. The only person she could get through to was her sister, Karen.

"Karen, it's me, Nance. I'm out and I'm okay," she said to the voicemail.

"Okay," she said resolutely after hanging up, "time to make plans." Her mind kicked into operational mode. "It's going to take us a long time to restore these towers and bring them back into service." She remembered how difficult it was to contact all the tenants after the 1993 bombing. The telephones were down then, and she was certain they were down now. Her plan was to get home and use the Internet to get a message to all the tenants via the new emergency notification system, let them know exactly what happened, and give them contact phone numbers.

Leaving the store, Nancy, Bob, and Nori Ishikawa, another coworker, began walking north on West Street, back toward the towers. Pausing at

Carlisle Street, the sound of a thousand colliding fast-moving freight trains attacked their ears.

"It's a third plane!" a nearby woman screamed.

###

9:45 A.M.

The parade of evacuees had been descending round and round for nearly an hour. Everyone had a handkerchief, or a jacket, or something covering his or her mouth and nose, so thick was the smoke. The unmistakable sounds of people falling on the stairs came from somewhere not far below. As Whitney Birch and Erik Ronningen reached the teen floors, water poured through the walls and cascaded down the steps like a waterfall. The steps had become slippery, and people nearing the end of the climb down were approaching exhaustion and becoming careless. *This is not a good time to have a broken leg*, Erik thought, reaching for the handrail. The evacuation was beginning to resemble an accordion as the exit onto the concourse level approached. The people massed as the progress ground to a stop. Erik took the opportunity to reach down and roll up his trouser legs. *Damn*, he thought to himself, *my brand new wing-tip shoes are soaking, and my feet are beginning to rub. I'll end up with a blister or two.*

Someone from above was getting impatient and began yelling, "What's the holdup? Get moving!"

"Works every time, Erik," Whitney mumbled.

"Step aside!" someone called out again. "Coming up!" More firemen and plainclothes policemen passed, and sure enough, after a minute or so, the crowd began moving again. *12 . . . 8 . . .*

###

"Sarah!" Diane exclaimed to Sarah Ronningen as she entered the Greenwich, Connecticut, office and saw her working at her desk. "Sarah! What are you doing here?" she asked, concerned. "I thought you would have gone home by now. The World Trade Center is under attack by terrorists!"

"It can't be that bad, Diane," Sarah responded quietly, countering Diane's excitability. She didn't feel as calm as she sounded. "Or else Erik would have called me by now."

"Which tower does he work in?" Diane asked.

"Oh, I don't know," Sarah answered hesitantly. "One . . . or maybe Two. I'm not really sure."

Jerry Dinkels met up with a Port Authority associate, Trish Cullen, a property manager with the World Trade Department. Trish was tired and needed a rest, and Jerry didn't object as they exited the stairs and entered the office spaces on the twenty-sixth floor. They ran into a group of people resting, all of whom Jerry knew—his boss, Achille Niro, and the chief architect among them—as well as a group of firemen who were taking a much-needed break.

Someone found bottled water and everyone was resting, drinking, and swapping stories about the morning. In Jerry's mind the emergency was over. Everyone was laid back, taking it easy. He tried calling his office and couldn't get past a dial tone. He tried calling his wife, Mary Ellen, to tell her that he was all right, but he couldn't get a connection.

"Did you know that another plane hit the building?" a fireman said, making casual conversation.

"What?" Jerry asked, hanging up the phone.

"Yeah, another plane hit the building a while ago."

Suddenly, Trish began weeping. She was standing next to Ezra Avales looking out the windows overlooking the roof of the Marriott Hotel.

"What?" Jerry asked again, immediately concerned. "What's the problem?"

"Jerry," Ezra stated, "there are dead people on the roof of the Marriott Hotel."

They were on the south side of the North Tower, about four floors higher up than the roof of the Marriott. Jerry looked down onto the roof and saw dead people. The others raced to the windows to have a look for themselves.

Jerry saw what appeared to be a young woman wearing a pink coral dress lying on her back in what, ironically, looked to him like a classic death pose.

"Oh no!" he exclaimed. *My God*, he thought, realizing the horror of it all. It occurred to him that this poor woman was in her office doing her job. *What more normal and secure environment is there than your workplace?* Jerry thought. And here was this poor woman sprawled out on the roof. *Dead!*

"We have jumpers!" a fireman yelled.

"Oh, my God!" Jerry said quietly to himself, the urgency of the situation dawning on him.

With a renewed sense of resolve, everyone turned toward the door and began scrambling for the stairwell—when suddenly there was a tremendous roar!

9:50 A.M.

"Hey, what are you doing up here?" a fireman immediately challenged Vic Guarnera when he exited the B-stairwell onto the twenty-second floor of the North Tower. "Where are you going?" another fireman confronted.

"My people are trapped in the Security Command Center," Vic responded. "I'm here to get them out."

"Okay," the fireman said. "Let me take you over there." As they approached the south corridor, Vic noticed that there was a gaping hole in the floor near the freight elevator shaft, and that the shaft was exposed. It was the wall separating the elevator from the approach to the Security Command Center that had collapsed into the sally-port entry, jamming it closed. Using his heavy-duty flashlight, the fireman guided Vic around the gaping black hole in the floor and away from the open shaft. Someone had arrived before Vic, as the debris, he noticed, had been cleared away from the entry, and he walked in.

There were extra people in the Security Command Center. In addition to Jitendra Mavadia, Jonesie, and Maria, Vic's friend and colleague George Tabeek had recently arrived. Tom Comerford from the technology department was there, as was FDNY Lieutenant Andy Desperito and an unknown FBI agent identifiable by his blue fleece jacket with the three large letters printed on the back. Vic conferred on the status of the command center and quickly concluded that the situation was not good.

He immediately released Maria, one of the security guards and a mother of young children, and she was escorted through the remains of the sally-port and around the gaping black hole in the floor outside the freight elevator, out to the stairwell.

The computer systems were not responding. He couldn't get a log-on screen for the building management system. There were additional problems with the security system because the operators were no longer able to command the system to turn the doors and turnstiles to the offline mode.

"S5, S1." It was Doug Karpiloff in the Operations Command Center in the S-1 basement level of the South Tower calling for Vic on the radio.

"S5. Go Doug," Vic responded.

"Transfer all control from the Operations Command Center to the Security Command Center on the twenty-second floor. The building management systems are not responding down here."

"Doug," Vic answered, "the systems aren't responding up here either. I'll keep working on them."

"Keep me posted," Doug instructed, signing off.

The telephones were working and Vic heard George Tabeek take a call from Alan Reiss, the director of the World Trade Department. Alan was at the police desk in Building Five and asked George to give him an assessment of Tower Two, the South Tower. Then Vic heard George say, "Stand by, Alan. I'll take a look out the windows and get right back to you."

The radio traffic was heavy and frenetic when a crackled message from someone got through, broadcasting that the South Tower was making funny noises.

9:52 A.M.

Erik Ronningen would have cheered had he had the energy when he exited the door leading onto the west concourse level, but when asked what floor he was from, all he could answer was "seventy-one." His body was numb from the hour-plus climb down, and his mind wasn't in much better shape.

At first all he could see were a hundred people formed up like two walls, and those exiting the C-stairwell were sandwiched between the human bulwarks. "Move quickly!" they all instructed with an urgency that was soon to become clear. As everyone quickly shuffled north and then east around the concourse level, the view out to the five-acre plaza— where the big, beautiful fountain and vendor kiosks were—suddenly, and with startling clarity, brought the shocking terror of the chaos taking place at ground level into vivid, horrifying focus.

"Keep moving quickly. Don't look outside!" came the commands of the guard force and police directing the evacuation of tens of thousands of employees.

Erik was taller than most and of course he looked. No thoughts passed through his numb mind as he took in the devastation. It was a scene from a Hollywood war motion picture set. Debris and bodies—bodies of every imaginable horrific appearance—were strewn about, not unlike the opening scenes of *Saving Private Ryan*. The plaza was totally unrecognizable.

"Keep moving quickly! Don't look outside!" was the chant of every guard urging everyone forward in the evacuation.

Erik recognized one of the guards at the head of the escalator leading down to the main lobby and stepped out of the line. "Do you know where Doug Karpiloff's last reported location was?" he asked.

A shrug was his reward for the question, and a mumbled "the Operations Command Center." It was answered more as a question.

Taking the opportunity to get an unobstructed view, Erik clearly saw the urgency of the situation. Someone—not on America's side—had planned to the nth degree and flawlessly executed the perfect terrorist attack on the World Trade Center. It was every facility and security manager's ultimate nightmare come true. *This cannot be happening*, Erik thought. How many conversations and planning sessions had there been over the years since February 1993, discussing the ways and means of preventing another attack on this complex? And yet, deep down, to a man, each privately knew someone was at work, diligently planning—because the last attempt was a failure—what was now taking place.

Erik walked over to the three-story windows overlooking the plaza. Not a foot over the other side of the blood-splattered glass were the remnants of a man gruesomely twisted like a pretzel. Moving his unbelieving eyes in a swath, back and forth, and out toward the plaza fountain, Erik registered dozens and dozens of bodies strewn about . . . as well as the debris of paper and trash and huge chunks of metal embedded into the terrazzo pavement.

Erik stood, his nose not three inches from the window, looking east toward the fountain. Suddenly, in the nanosecond it takes to blink an eye, time froze as a man plummeting at a hundred miles per hour and Erik made solid eye contact. The next nanosecond tick of the clock brought the sudden shotgun sound of his body hitting the ground, exploding as it went from a hundred miles per hour to instant zero. His bodily fluids sprayed in every direction; fresh blood flowed down the window. Numb, Erik redoubled his resolve to help his friend Doug Karpiloff. He turned to continue his journey to the Operations Command Center in the basement of the South Tower.

Walking down the no-longer-running escalator brought another shock. The main lobby was a disaster. The beautiful, giant crystal chandeliers were in heaps on the floor, the marble walls were in broken piles, and the massive directional signage dangled from the ceiling by a cable. The giant plateglass windows were shattered and strewn about, the revolving doors were busted and all off-kilter, and the elevator doors in the B-corridor were blown out of their frames. *What in God's name has caused all this devastation?* Erik thought. It was too much for any sane man to take in.

As he stepped off the escalator onto the main lobby floor there was another blow and more water, up to the ankles. The guard force was funneling everyone out of the towers through the darkened mall. The falling water sounded like Niagara Falls as everyone waded east past the coffee station. The waterfall was pounding down, and there was a moment of hesitation as people tested their ability to breathe under the force of the cascading falls.

"Keep moving, quickly!" the guards commanded, great urgency in their voices. They had continued the human wall, funneling everyone out through the distance of the unlit mall.

9:54 A.M.

Sarah Ronningen's coffee had run its course, and as she approached the sinks in the ladies room, she encountered a lady in tears, crying uncontrollably. "Are you okay? May I help you?" Sarah inquired.

"I have . . ." she sobbed, "I have . . . family . . . down there."

"You have family down . . . where?" Sarah asked cautiously, dreading the only obvious answer.

"At the . . . World Trade Center." She broke down with her statement, unable to bear the reality of it all. "We have . . ." she said, stumbling over her words, "we have a . . . television," she finally managed to get out. "Would you . . . would you like to come . . . and see?" she inquired, sniffling.

The progress down from Yvonne Barker's eighty-sixth-floor office began to bog. Stop and go. Some of the people began to express their impatience.

Yvonne was not inexperienced with difficult situations. Growing up in a tough neighborhood, she quickly learned how to fight her own battles, and she knew how to handle herself. But the strain, exhaustion, heat, and smoke were beginning to have their adverse effects. This situation, she had to admit to herself, far exceeded anything she had had to endure in her youth.

"Thank God," she mumbled to herself as she stepped through the door leading into the mezzanine level, right near the escalator that went down into the main lobby. She saw Ernesto Butcher and Jeff Green assisting people. The escalator was stopped and they were helping people get started down the first few steps.

"Don't look!" someone shouted. "Don't look out into the plaza!" They were telling everybody to just keep going down the escalator and not to look at the plaza.

Telling Yvonne "don't" was an engraved invitation, so of course she looked.

"My God!" she exclaimed. "What's going on?" The plaza was a mess of debris, rocks, metal, glass . . . and little piles of clothing. And it appeared to be snowing paper.

"Keep moving!" the voice commanded. She dragged her eyes away from the plaza and stepped onto the escalator. Ernesto held her elbow to support her for her first awkward step down, and she walked, hands on the rail for support, to the bottom unaided. Turning left at the bottom, she walked through what once were the revolving doors—it was a little puzzling to her how she could just walk through—into the mall and stopped by the coffee station on her left.

"Thank God we made it!" There was such jubilation. "Oh, we made it!" Everyone was hugging one another; some were kissing—so wonderful was the freedom from the all-encompassing claustrophobic containment of the stairwells.

Looking into the mall, she could see that it was completely deserted, like when she worked late after everyone had gone home. *Serene even*, she thought. All the stores were closed. Everything was locked up. And a steady stream of people filed down the middle, splitting, some to exit at Vesey Street halfway down on the left, others onto Church Street at the far end.

"Oh, God," Yvonne commented to Flory, ever the gentleman. "I am so tired." He had escorted her the whole way down. "I am so, so tired," she repeated. Her whole body shook from fatigue and exhaustion. Her only thought was to get out of the mall and onto the street.

It was just a couple more minutes to freedom, sunshine, and fresh air. For the first time, as they stepped off into the future, Yvonne noticed that they were walking hand-in-hand.

The worst was behind them . . .

Tad Hanc arrived at the twenty-second floor and exited into the office spaces to take a breather. He bumped into his coworker George Tabeek who worked for the Port Authority's World Trade Department.

"Tad, Tad," George called out. "What happened? Do you know what happened?"

"Well, yeah! I had seen a plane hitting the building," Tad answered, his Polish accent evident in the mayhem.

"No kidding, no kidding!" George responded. "Well, this is something. Why don't you tell what you saw, and describe it to this FBI agent right here?"

"Fine." As Tad began to describe his experience watching the plane fly directly into his office, he noticed the FBI agent searching, with no success, for a piece of paper and a pen. "Listen, sir," Tad suggested, "why don't you go with me downstairs to your headquarters, and I can put my story to paper?"

The agent agreed that this was a good idea, and they continued the climb down together. As they reached the fourteenth floor, suddenly there was a huge explosion and the tower shook like it was in an earthquake—and then the lights went out.

9:55 A.M.

"Would you . . . would you like to come . . . and see?" the woman at the washbasin sobbingly repeated.

Sarah Ronningen looked at the distraught woman standing next to her in the ladies room, trying to decide whether to accept her offer to watch the events unfold on her office television. A feeling of dread descended upon Sarah. Internal alarms began to sound. The intent of the telephone calls from her best friend, Liz Kelly, counseling her to come and stay with her and Jackie, was coming home to roost.

"Yes," Sarah answered, knowing in her heart that it was not going to be an easy matter.

Erik Ronningen approached the darkened Banana Republic and the mall corridor leading south to Tower Two, shouldering his way through the bulwark of guards.

"Hey! Get back in line! You can't go past here!" the guard said, not all too kindly.

"Security! Coming through," he blustered, just as unkindly. "I'm going to the Operations Command Center." No further resistance was given as he headed south. The walk was a lonely one. Wading through ankle-deep water, the sounds of waterfalls and shouting guards directing the evacuation faded into the distance. The corridor was dark and there was no activity in the main lobby of Tower Two. All thoughts of Whitney Birch had long been forgotten since they became separated at the top of the escalator. There was only one goal: get to the Operations Command Center in the basement of Tower Two.

"Excuse me, please," Erik commandingly informed a group of firemen and police officers blocking the door to the left of the Ben & Jerry's ice cream kiosk. That was the door that led down to the sub-grades, the basements under Tower Two. "Coming through. Going down here," he blustered.

"Hold it, mister!" an NYPD officer commanded, raising his arms to block his passage. "You can't go down there. Get out of the building, now!"

The officer was only performing his job. All he saw was a businessman in his late fifties wearing black wing-tip shoes, dressed in a pinstripe suit with the trousers rolled up to his knees, dripping with water as if he had just climbed out of a swimming pool, soaking black briefcase in his hand, wet graying hair matted down over his face.

"Security," Erik countered using his military voice. "I'm with World Trade Center Security heading down to my post in the Operations Command Center. I'm with Doug Karpiloff, Director of Security and Life Safety."

Erik was no stranger to commanding men and having his orders followed. He had attended four years at the Valley Forge Military Academy and College and had been the commander of his unit the year he graduated in 1966, receiving his commission. As a captain in the United States Army Corps of Engineers, Erik had served in Germany commanding a NATO facility in the Fulda Gap. And as a project manager for many years in private industry, he had been responsible for obtaining results from the New York City local labor unions. Erik was not intimidated by authority or threats or bullying. And he was not intimidated now. He had a destination, and he was going to attain that destination: the Operations Command Center located in the sub-level basement of Tower Two.

"May I see some identification, sir?" the officer grudgingly asked.

Erik reached into his right jacket pocket and pulled out his mahogany, calfskin leather World Trade Center identification case. "This is my World Trade Center access identification," he said, showing the officer his yellow badge, "and this is my Port Authority identification," he added, displaying the white Port Authority photo identification card.

"All right, sir," the officer consented, "but you'll have to wait until we get some equipment up, out of the stairwell."

Helena Marietta was exhausted. After clambering out of the elevator and trying to exit the maze of the equipment room, she found some back stairs and carefully climbed down. She was puzzled that she didn't see anyone else, but she kept going until she got to a door. Her bare feet were getting sore, but she pressed on. She opened the door and found herself in another equipment or locker room of some sort. She found another door and walked down another long flight of stairs.

Helena opened another door and stepped into a large, cavernous area. It was nearly dark with water up above her ankles. Her feet were killing her, protected only by her pantyhose. She had lost her shoes in the elevator. Helena began wading through the cave and suddenly recognized that she was in the mall. Trying to hurry her exhausted body and now blistering feet to an exit, she tripped over a pile of something soft. She didn't stop, even though she knew that something else she had stepped on had cut her feet. The light of an exit out of the mall and onto the street was within range, and Helena was anxious to get out.

9:56 A.M.

Impatient for activity, and not wishing to invest any more time waiting for the firemen to clear the stairwell at the entrance to the sub-grade basement leading to the command center, Erik Ronningen struck out for an alternative entrance further east in the facility. To avoid additional sloshing through ankle-deep water, he clambered through the broken revolving doors into the north-side lobby of Tower Two.

"What in the world has happened here?" Erik mumbled to himself. "This place looks just like Tower One." He now suspected that the announcement from the lady wearing the Sony Walkman that "another plane has hit the towers" was accurate. When he walked the width of the lobby his worst fears were confirmed.

Something else here is odd, Erik thought. *There is no one in the main lobby, not even evacuating employees. No one.* The place was deserted. It was like New York City had been evacuated for twenty years. No one was at the visitor desk all the way to the south windows; no one was in the B-corridor elevator lobby; no one was visible at the Fire Command Center . . .

Where is everybody? he wondered.

The eerie silence was deafening, save for the incessant groaning and grinding sounds resonating, emanating, from somewhere deep within the tower.

The walk from the ladies room through the law firm's lobby and into the partner's office took Sarah Ronningen less than a minute. The forty-two-inch-wide, flat-screen television was mounted on the wall to afford everyone a clear, unobstructed view. Half the people in the firm must have been in there watching, and when Sarah entered and looked . . . her mind and body froze.

Gabriella Ballini, more exhausted than she could ever remember being, at long last exited the never-ending confines of circular stairs packed with people. She walked to the right, and then around to the escalator on the other side of the mezzanine, never once looking beyond the head of the person in front of her. The escalator wasn't working, so it was just another flight of "bend the right knee, put the right foot down on the next step, bend the left knee . . ." How many thousands of times had she done this in the past hour or so? One more flight. *It doesn't matter*, she told herself. *Just keep going.*

In her complete exhaustion, Gabriella thought she saw water covering the lobby floor. Totally mystified, she stepped off the final stair of the escalator—into water over her ankles! The whole side of the building had revolving doors going into the mall, but today she just sloshed through, pushing nothing.

The cops and firemen were directing people to hurry through. "Go this way, quickly!" they shouted, pointing. "Keep going. Don't look back!" they commanded. Gabriella was jogging, struggling to keep up, struggling to keep from slipping. She noticed that all the stores in the mall were empty, closed, doors locked. The place looked like a graveyard. Except for the evacuees in one large stream pouring toward an exit on Vesey Street, there was nobody around.

Gabriella fervently hoped she would see her husband and children again.

Rounding the corner at The Gap, near the escalators and stairs leading down to the PATH Station, the world as Gabriella Ballini knew it changed forever.

###

9:57 A.M.

Time stood still for Sarah Ronningen. She tried to comprehend the enormity of what she was seeing. CNN first showed the plane crashing into Tower One, with the resultant explosions, and then the second plane circling around and flying into Tower Two. And then a real-time shot of both towers. Ravaging fires were burning in the tops of both towers, billowing flames and smoke high into the air, with fragments of the towers falling off, and . . . "Oh, no! There are people jumping out of the building!" someone who had just entered yelled.

Everyone in the room was screaming. Sarah couldn't believe her eyes! Her husband, Erik, was down there somewhere. Her knees weakened. The realization came to her that she didn't know which tower he worked in, or what floor he worked on.

It can't get any worse than this, she thought. She stood there, supported by the edge of a desk, immobile and frozen. The bile of nausea manufactured itself from deep within her system. She was unable to take her eyes off the unfolding scenes taking place on the television set.

Erik Ronningen found himself back in the empty, dark, flooded mall sloshing northeast when he was apprehended by yet another group of NYPD officers. Not to be deterred in his mission, he adroitly parried their verbal thrusts and continued heading toward where he knew he would be able to get down under Tower Two to the Operations Command Center.

9:58 A.M.

From the twenty-second floor of Tower One, Vic Guarnera had just completed his radio transmission with Doug Karpiloff in the basement Operations Command Center of Tower Two. He joined George Tabeek and they both walked over to the windows overlooking the Marriott Hotel, to look out and up at the South Tower to make their appraisal for Alan Reiss.

"Thank goodness Tower Two is in good shape," George said to Vic.

Unable to explain how it happened, Erik Ronningen discovered that he was back with the evacuating employees walking out of the mall and up the escalators to the Church Street exit in Building Five. The guard force had continued the human cordon, funneling people out of the buildings and across Church Street.

The outdoor sounds were a cacophony of disorder and confusion. *Good God, look at all these people!* Erik observed. Thousands of them were evacuating the buildings; thousands and thousands were standing around, watching. And thousands more were running . . .

"Move-a-way-from-the-build-ings!" the guard force kept yelling at everyone, punctuating each syllable. "And don't look up! Keep mov-ing!" they commanded as people stopped to turn and look up, slowing down the evacuation.

At Church Street, Erik stepped out of the river of evacuees, stopped, and turned around. And looked up. "Wha—!?" His numb brain faltered. *I don't believe what my eyes are showing me!* he exclaimed to himself. Both towers were burning, the top thirds of which were fully engaged in flames and billowing smoke. Debris was all over the place. The sight more than confirmed the second plane announcement he had heard in the stairwell while descending Tower One over an hour ago. "I was just in there," he exclaimed to himself. "Unbelievable!"

Erik's natural inclination was to stick around and provide a service, to help. He had seen the carnage in the plaza when he stood at the concourse windows of Tower One. Briefcase in hand, Erik stepped off in military fashion and marched south toward the plaza entrance to provide whatever assistance he could. When he was perpendicular to Fulton Street, a life-changing event occurred.

Through the din of a thousand shouting voices, Erik heard a quiet voice in his head command, *walk east.* In his weakened physical and mental condition he was in no shape to argue, and like a good soldier, when his right foot came into contact with the intersecting pavement of Church Street, he obeyed the command. He executed a left-flank movement and stepped off, walking east up Fulton Street, away from the towers.

V

Collapse

9:59 A.M.

Captain Anthony Whitaker's chief approached him. They were at West and Vesey Streets. There were hundreds of FDNY firemen, all in their bunker gear, awaiting instructions. The scene was a disaster: debris, bodies, fire trucks, EMS equipment, and hundreds of other first responders. "Let's take a walk," the chief said to Tony. He wanted to get a little privacy—a little quiet time with his captain. As they approached West Broadway, Tony heard another thunderous explosion. "Oh, hell, that isn't good," he said out loud to himself. "More people are going to get killed."

Eyes glued to the unfolding horror on the television set, suddenly it felt as if a fist had punched Sarah Ronningen hard in her solar plexus. Her breathing stopped, and she watched the sudden and totally unexpected collapse of Tower Two, the South Tower. Sarah's knees gave way and she sank to the floor, holding on to the desk for balance. Everyone in the office began screaming hysterically, in total disbelief of what they were witnessing.

Sarah's mind became a numb object over which she no longer had command. It presented her with a sudden realization—her life's absolute worst fear—the prospect of having to live out her remaining days without her husband, Erik. "Where *is* he!?" she wailed.

"Where is all that blood coming from?" Erik Ronningen asked himself as he began marching east on Fulton Street, away from the towers. He looked down at the pavement and saw many bloody footprints, their fresh marks running east.

Suddenly the earth began to vibrate. The pavement shook with a violence that only an earthquake could produce and he feared the street was going to collapse beneath him into the subway tunnels. Erik turned toward the accompanying volcanic rumbling roar; the tens of thousands of rubbernecking spectators were propelled into instant action. They began to stampede in every direction away from the danger, like buffalo in a prairie fire.

Erik uttered no expletives as he maintained his position and witnessed what could just as well have been an IMAX movie: the collapse of Tower Two. "This really isn't happening, is it?" he mumbled to himself, not believing what his eyes were showing him. The reality of the situation—the noise, the panic, and the shrapnel from the imploding tower—was confirmation enough. It *was* happening.

In absolute panic people flooded the streets. Everyone was racing, charging away from the danger in a mad rout. Everywhere Erik looked people were running, arms flailing, screaming, wailing . . .

"That explains the blood," he said to himself as he sidestepped a panic-stricken woman barreling down upon him, barefoot, her bloody footprints leaving their mark.

The thought of the tower coming down upon him flashed through his mind, and in that instant he feared that it was. In the same instant, a calmness came over him with the realization that if it did, it did; it would be his time to go. Erik's natural instinct was to run, too. *But where can you run to escape a quarter-mile-high structure?* he thought.

For whatever reason, Erik had always known how important it was not to get caught up in the animal mentality of panicking crowds of people. So, to avoid being run down by the terrified hordes, and to protect himself from the deadly shrapnel exploding through the air, he matched his walking/running speed to that of the panicking mob and maneuvered to the side of the nearest building, the Millennium Hotel. It had structural columns on the outside, on the sidewalk, and he tucked himself behind one of them by the loading dock doors.

The danger of shrapnel quickly passed, but the human stampede with all the screaming and flailing of arms continued. Erik looked into the street and saw high-heeled shoes and loafers being kicked about by the thousands of feet slamming the pavement, carrying their panicking owners away, running out of their shoes. He tentatively stepped out from his temporary protection, and turned west to return to the World Trade Center to provide whatever help he could.

"Run!" thousands of voices began yelling.

But everyone is already running, he confirmed.

The monstrous mob took up the chant, and now thousands more were running again, and yelling, "Run! Run for your lives!" The already-panicking stampede had renewed its focus and determination.

One look and Erik froze in place. An eight-hundred-foot-high tidal wave of broiling, black cloud replaced the collapsed tower. Already exhausted, both mentally and physically, this new horror was over-whelming and threatened to tax him beyond endurance. *Will I survive this day?* he asked himself. *How many more of these horrors can I survive?*

The outcome was uncertain.

Walk east, said that quiet voice in his head.

Vic Guarnera and George Tabeek were looking out of the twenty-second-floor window of the Security Command Center, up at the west face of the South Tower.

"Look, George," Vic said. "There is a hole in the west wall two or three floors high and maybe twelve to fifteen windows wide."

"No. It can't be!" George exclaimed.

"Yeah. Come on over here."

"Naw," George replied, "I don't see anything."

"Yes, look up!" Vic insisted. "Look up to about the seventy-eighth floor."

Vic and George were looking up at the top of the South Tower when they heard it snap and saw it rotate, as if a giant hand had pushed it. The top of the tower—accompanied by the roar of the Concord accelerating down the runway, or an avalanche—began to fall onto the roof of the Marriott Hotel. The roar increased, and immediately all visibility was obscured by a thick, dark cloud.

It's terrorists, Vic concluded. *They've just blown off the top of the South Tower!* The debris was exploding through the glass windows in front of them, but the bulletproof glass recently installed inside the Security Command Center held firm. Vic tried to process the fact that the entire South Tower was, in all probability, collapsing. He turned back into the room and yelled, "Let's get the hell out of here!"

"Lieutenant," Vic said to FDNY Lieutenant Andy Desperito, "Lieutenant, issue the command to evacuate the tower."

This took a little convincing. In the history of the FDNY, it had never issued an evacuation of a building. The order was also beyond Lieutenant Desperito's authority to issue. Vic was well versed in incident command procedures, the guidelines and procedures used in all emergency situations. And though he was in a suit, his wealth of experience gained in the military and in civilian search-and-rescue operations expressed itself in his comportment. He instructed the lieutenant that the lieutenant was an officer, that the lieutenant understood the current dire circumstances, and that at the very least the lieutenant should inform his superiors that they should order a withdrawal from the tower.

Lieutenant Desperito understood the wisdom in the order. As he lifted the radio to his lips, the order to evacuate was broadcast by his chief: "Evacuate Building One and clear out!" was the command repeated three or four times.

Nancy Seliga, Bob Benacchio, and Nori Ishikawa, having just run out of the South Tower toward Battery Park, turned around and were walking north on West Street, back toward the towers, when the sound of a thousand colliding freight trains attacked their ears. As one they immediately turned and ran south, back toward Battery Park. Those thousand freight trains were hard on their heels. Like Lot's wife, the temptation was too great for Nancy not to look and see what was happening. She twisted her head around.

"Oh, my God!" Nancy yelled. She was not praying. She had just seen the end of life as she knew it. Her legs couldn't pump any harder. "Run, run, run!" she heard herself screaming, panting for air. In an instant, the world turned black. A black, windy, gritty cloud enveloped her and the entire world, wrapping itself around everything and everyone. Her legs kept pumping. She couldn't see anything, though she did hear children screaming, and then instant silence. For the briefest flash of time she hoped this was a nightmare and that her alarm would go off.

Nancy couldn't see, couldn't breathe, and couldn't run another step, yet she knew that if there was ever a time for extraordinary effort, this was it. Since 1993, Nancy had had asthma, and the grit that was now packed up her nose and in her throat wasn't helping her desperate medical condition. She couldn't breathe.

Through the darkness, Nancy heard a familiar voice call her name. It was Bob Benacchio. He had stopped at a little pond of water at the Holocaust Museum. They were near Battery Park. The water was filthy and black, but it didn't matter. As did the others around her, Nancy immediately scooped it up in the palms of her hands and threw it on her face.

The black, malevolent cloud hid the sun. With great difficulty Nancy looked around and, through the grit-laden atmosphere, saw people knock over hot dog carts to get at the water, to splash it into their eyes and to drink. She couldn't believe she was still alive.

Nori Ishikawa had disappeared. Nancy and Bob continued trudging south, through Battery Park and up the east side toward the South Street Seaport. They just kept walking and walking. The gray fallout was everywhere. Nancy's black heels matched her dress, which had turned from beige to sooty gray. The gray city camouflaged her.

Gabriella Ballini was jubilant. She had made it to the mall after climbing down from the eighty-second floor, and she was going to see her family again. She was rounding the corner at The Gap, by the escalator bank going down to the PATH subway station. Then, in the blink of an eye, Gabriella's life went into slow motion. In that split second, time became an eternity. Gabriella felt a gigantic crushing pressure instantly build from somewhere behind her. In that same terrifying flash, a paralyzing fear seized her mind, preventing all thought. Gabriella was trapped. She no longer had any control over events in her life. She thought her ears were going to explode as the pressure increased. The simultaneous, unrelenting thunderous eruption continued to crescendo.

All time stopped. Boom! Boom! Boom! The deafening staccato pressure waves were swelling. As if from a catapult, Gabriella was launched into the air. She was flying, arms outstretched, rotating uncontrollably. She saw everybody flying! Twirling, tumbling, twisting people smashed into one another. In her mind's eye was the image of a strike in bowling; the people looked like the pins shooting into the air. Gabriella's airborne body was bombarded with shrapnel. She could see that the store windows had exploded and glass and debris were competing for airspace. In the same instant of time since the pressure began an infinity ago, the lights went out. Darkness emerged from behind, racing the airborne wreckage at the speed of sound past her—darkness she could only imagine existing six feet under. The thunderous, deafening roar was perpetual, the darkness complete, and she was flying like a bird with a broken wing through a hurricane.

Yvonne Barker and Flory Danish walked hand-in-hand from the coffee station, past the portion of the mall leading directly to the South Tower, and approached the near end of the Banana Republic.

"Oh, God! What now?" Yvonne screamed. That instant fear she had experienced in her office when the tower first shook and the ceilings fell down, that same deafening, horrible sound, attacked her again. She jerked her head to the right, toward the South Tower, and saw a monstrous black cloud of smoke and what looked like tangled building material swarming at her like a flash flood. At the same time she felt Flory's grip tighten like a vice and yank her to the protection of the north wall of the Banana Republic.

They started running. Yvonne slipped and fell. Water was everywhere. Flory tried to pull her to her feet. An explosion deafened her, and then everything went black, blinding. The air around her was so thick—and powerful. Suddenly, it was like a huge hand reached under her, picked up her body, and shot her through the air. She understood what it must feel to be a human cannonball at the circus. For what seemed like forever, she flopped, and spun, and turned in slow motion through the black, deafening space.

Yvonne came to on her knees. Her vision was blackness; her hearing was nonexistent. She was utterly alone in an unknown place. She had no idea where she was, or what had happened to bring her to this . . . place. She wasn't breathing. She couldn't even feel her body. She felt just like . . . consciousness . . . floating.

Slowly, ever so slowly, the dim light of realization began to seep into the edges of her rational mind. It was truly frightening, but she now knew beyond a doubt the terribleness of her condition—she was dead!

Yvonne was a religious woman. She went to church, prayed, sang the hymns, and tithed as best she could. She believed in Jesus and had faith in what her minister preached. She believed that when she died she would have a place at Jesus's side.

She didn't see any welcoming Jesus to walk with her and to talk with her. Could it be that she had been deceived all these years? If anything, it looked like she was in the reception hall of hell.

Yvonne's mind began trying to pull her situation together. She sat there, listening—and didn't hear a sound—and looking—and couldn't see a thing. She called out for Flory, but couldn't tell if any sound came out of her mouth. She wasn't even certain that she had tried calling his name.

Then slowly, ever so slowly, she began to hear. Everything sounded muffled, hushed, subdued. Her sight began to come back, hazy. She realized that she was on her knees, and began to feel all around her body to see if everything was in its proper place, the way she remembered it ought to be. There was water everywhere! There was grit in her mouth and her skin felt oily. Now she knew that she was not dead, but that knowledge only redoubled her fear.

She had lost her flats, and began feeling all around for them. But all she could feel were big chunks of glass . . . and people, and parts of people. She quickly gave up the idea of finding her shoes, keeping her hands to herself. She was afraid to move, not knowing if there was any floor in front of her. There was a dark shape hanging over her, but she didn't know what it was. So she just stayed where she was, trying to figure out what she should do.

Yvonne was a practical person, and she liked the practical aspects of her religion. She didn't know what to do, but she knew that He would know.

Dear God, she began to pray, *what should I do?* After a short pause, she continued. *God,* she implored, *what should I do? Should I stay here? Or should I move? You have brought me this far.*

"If you can see the light, come to the light," a man's voice immediately boomed through the darkness and gloom.

Thank you, Jesus! Yvonne's prayer was answered.

"Form a human chain and come to the light. I'll get you out," the voice instructed.

Tad Hanc and the FBI agent were going to the FBI's office so Tad could dictate his experience watching the American airliner fly directly toward the tower. They had just reached the fourteenth floor when suddenly there was a huge explosion and the tower shook as though in an earthquake. The lights went out and they were in complete and total darkness. Tad could hear a rush of wind coming from the lower floors and a lot of commotion. "Go up! Go up! Run, run, run!" People were beginning to panic. It was so dark people didn't know which way to go. They were shouting and running in different directions. Fortunately, Tad had had the foresight to take his flashlight when he left his office an eternity ago, and he used it to guide people up to the next landing and through the door leading to the offices.

For some reason, Tad kept finding the right unlocked doors, and using his flashlight, he directed people through the pitch-dark corridors, passing them off to someone else with a flashlight, like racers in a marathon relay race. He found another stairwell and led the way down. It was so hot; the dust and dirt were so thick that Tad wrapped his undershirt around his face, tying it off. And down he continued to lead his blinded, suffocating flock of followers.

Captain Anthony Whitaker heard another thunderous explosion and knew beyond a doubt that more people were going to get killed. The doors leading to the truck loading docks of WTC Building #7 were to his left, and with everything Tony had left in him, he ran for his life. He was catapulted into the tunnel leading to the docks and, as he was pushed down the concrete driveway, he grabbed onto a column. But two other men had already claimed it, so he grabbed onto their bodies and held on for dear life. Day immediately turned into black night, and the ninety-mile-per-hour wind forced sand and grit into his mouth. It was pitch dark when he stood up to gain his bearings and ran into, he thought, a woman. He helped her back outdoors. Someone grabbed him and dragged him to a bathroom in another building. Tony didn't recognize himself when he looked into a mirror. He was gray like a ghost. He threw some water onto his face and left, heading back to West Street.

Looking out at the Marriott Hotel roof from the twenty-sixth floor of Tower One, a fireman yelled, "We have jumpers!"—when suddenly there was a tremendous roar.

Jerry Dinkels thought some of the tower floors were coming down on them. The groan of the structure sounded like a train as it roared past, the floors shaking. Jerry looked up and noticed that the lights were blinking, flickering. Looking out the windows, the roar increased to unbearable levels as he watched in horror what he thought was the top of Tower One falling down past them. The unbelievable roar sounded like it came from directly overhead.

"What is that?" Achille Niro yelled, mesmerized, eyes magnetized to the thick cloud of smoke that totally obscured Tower Two, not comprehending the magnitude of all the metal and debris rushing past, some ricocheting off and breaking the windows.

"Get out of here!" Achille yelled. "Let's go!"

"Jerry!" Ezra yelled. "Get in the core!"

Jerry, not easily shaken, had to admit to himself that he was now a little more than anxious as he clambered along with everyone else through the darkened offices heading toward the core of the tower and the stairwells.

"Where's the guy in the wheelchair?" Jerry asked, recalling that on the way into the offices he had seen him. It was dark and smoky in the core, and Jerry also thought he had seen some of the firemen fall.

"He's right in back of us with his friend," someone answered through the smoke.

"Hey, chief?" Jerry said, recognizing a fire chief as he passed him. "Hey, chief? I think some of your men are down."

"I got it!" the chief replied as he disappeared into the darkness and smoke.

"I have to go to the bathroom again," Trish announced, running towards the ladies room.

"Go! Go!" Jerry commanded, holding the door open for her. He stood there with the door open for what seemed an eternity, and in that moment he thought of his family. Impatient at Trish's delay, and now fearful for his own life, he yelled, "Trish, what are you doing?"

"I have to wash my hands," she answered.

"Forget about your hands!" Jerry ordered. "Let's get out of here!"

Jerry and Trish found a stairwell through the darkened smoke and began to descend into the blackness. It was thick, black, caustic smoke, and breathing was difficult. Jerry had his arm around Trish's waist, holding, supporting, her. She was crying in the acrid blackness. Jerry gasped in short, sharp intakes of smoke. He couldn't breathe. The acid in the air stung his eyes and he couldn't open them. One arm around Trish, the other hand grasping the handrail for guidance, Jerry tried to enter into the office space on another floor hoping to get some fresh air. The doors were locked. He lost all track of which floors he was passing going down. Desperate, Jerry pulled his shirt and jacket over his face hoping to filter some of the smoke to get a little oxygen. Inhaling, gasping for air, all that entered was acrid smoke.

For the first time, Jerry was cognizant of the very real possibility of dying.

Helena Marietta was the happiest Montanan in New York City. Somehow she had survived a plummeting elevator, escaped from the tallest building in the city, waded through the dark, flooded mall, and was now standing safely on Liberty Street, with Church Street not far to her left. There was a man standing to her right, and as she turned to ask him why there were thousands of people—more people than she'd ever seen before—milling and gawking about, Helena heard the sound of hell opening up and exploding. The earth shook, the sun disappeared, and the thousands of people began to scream and move as one. As she tried to speak, her question froze in her mouth. A harpoon of metal impaled the man standing to her right. It went into his back and stuck a foot out his front.

Helena Marietta leapt into the crowd and became one of her daddy's Montana mares amongst the thousands stampeding away from the collapsing South Tower.

10:00 A.M.

Gabriella Ballini had been flying through the thunderous, black hurricane in the mall. Now, as swiftly as her flight began an eternity ago, it came to an abrupt end as she crash-landed and slid into a column. Another body crashed, smashing into hers, sliding away. She couldn't tell whether her eyes were open or closed, it was so black. Deathly silence surrounded her, as if she were lying on a cold marble slab in the crypt of a mausoleum. Gabriella tried to swallow, but the attempt was a failure. Something was in her mouth, gritty, awful. She didn't know what it was, but it was in her shoes, her underwear, everywhere. She was caked with the stuff. She tried to breathe . . . and there was water. Her face was in water!

I don't know where I am, Gabriella thought, panicking. *I don't believe it! I'm not going to make it!* Gabriella was terrified. She tried to pull herself together—and then she became aware of lots of smoke.

By sheer force of determination, Sarah Ronningen stood up and tore herself away from the television broadcasting the horrifying scenes of the South Tower collapsing—scenes that would forever imbue her memory and consciousness. She wandered, dazed and unnoticed, from the law offices back down the hall. She entered her office and one of her colleagues, Diane, stood facing her. No longer able to control the overwhelming emotion that had built up within her, Sarah burst into tears. She just stood there as Diane approached and gave her a big, sisterly hug.

"I'm leaving for the day," Sarah announced, sobbing. "I'm going to spend the day with my girlfriend, Liz, at Jackie Karpiloff's house. If—Erik—ca-calls—" she stuttered, tears dripping down her chin onto a piece of paper she was scribbling on, "if anyone calls with any information about Erik, I can be reached at this number." With soaked, red eyes she handed the tear-streaked piece of paper to Diane, gathered up her pocketbook, and in a daze walked down to the parking garage.

"Run!" the thousands of voices began to yell again. The mob was stampeding again, and in Erik Ronningen's complete, absolute horror and pure fascination, this new danger held him momentarily riveted in place. Head tilted back, he was unable to pull his eyes off that eight-hundred-foot-high, monstrous, intensifying gray-black cloud that erupted through the canyon walls of downtown New York City.

The image of Mount Pinatubo in the Philippines flashed before his mind's eye, with that stupendous pyroclastic cloud from the volcanic explosion. So, Erik thought, *I'm going to find out what it's like to get caught in that thing.*

He was jarred out of his macabre fascination by the pounding, stampeding panic as it increased all around him. Once again he heard that quiet little voice in his head instruct him to walk east. Erik did so as quickly as he could. The hordes were passing him by, but he knew how easy it was to get emotionally caught up in the panic, and what dangers that condition presented. Exercising all his will to keep from running, he forced himself to walk very quickly near the sides of the buildings, and attempted to enter each store he passed, hoping to escape the impending incarceration in that evil cloud. But to no avail. To his disbelief, every door was locked! All the merchants had long since closed up their shops and departed their premises.

With an urgency borne of desperation, Erik's cramping thighs and legs somehow continued to carry him eastward. Glancing over his shoulder, he looked up and saw the incredible, massive cloud of pulverized concrete, asbestos, glass—and what not. It was about to swallow up everyone in its path, like a gigantic avalanche bursting through California's fabled Donner Pass.

Dear Lord, Erik hastily prayed, *please give me the strength to deal with this.* At the same time, he acknowledged the answer received to his earlier prayer in the stairwell on the seventy-first floor, and added *thank you* to express his gratitude for the help received to get down all those stairs.

Then it hit; that ugly, hideous cloud punched him forward like the leading edge of a force-five gale. An instant before, Erik took a deep breath and held it. And the most amazing thing happened: the sound of running feet, the screaming, the wailing—all of it stopped.

Suddenly he was alone standing in a desert. Absolute silence reigned. His vision was nothing but deep, dark gray-blackness. *I can't even see my hand,* he thought to himself, pressing the palm of his right hand up to his nose and mouth.

Erik's first thought was to run and hide from this nightmare. *But how does one hide when he is already caught?* he wondered. The stronger thought was *walk east.* He didn't know if he was going to be run down by a truck, trip over a curb, stomp on prostrate bodies, or what . . . walking east was his only mission.

The grit, held in suspension by the tumultuous physics produced by the collapse, and thick as sand in a Sahara desert windstorm, had collected around his eyelids and frozen his eyes open.

After a minute or so, Erik's already-tortured body was screaming for oxygen. Breathing, a heretofore simple routine—a natural function taken so for granted—suddenly turned into his most pressing anxiety. He opened his mouth and attempted to inhale. It felt like someone had thrown a shovel of sand into his mouth. *There is no oxygen in a thick, pyroclastic-like cloud of pulverized concrete, asbestos, glass—and what not. If there is,* he concluded, *it isn't getting into my lungs.* His attempts to inhale resulted in a double column of impacted grit blocking all pathways through his nose. The grit—so dry that it made Death Valley dirt seem absolutely thirst-quenching—collected in all his pores and absorbed any remaining moisture, swelling his tongue and cinching his esophagus. Erik couldn't breathe! He thought for certain he was going to meet his Maker.

This is not the way I envisioned leaving this world, Erik thought. *I do not wish to die on a New York street I don't even know the name of.*

###

"Let's get the hell out of here!" Vic Guarnera repeated. In the twenty-second-floor Security Command Center, the sound of Tower Two's collapse was reverberating in everyone's ears. The FDNY order to evacuate Tower One issued, Systems Administrator Jitendra Mavadia reached into his file drawer and pulled out two flashlights, handing one off. With the aid of the flashlights everyone safely navigated around the black, gaping hole, through the corridor, and into the slightly smoky B-stairwell. Joining others evacuating, they carefully began the long, forty-four-flight climb down. At each floor, Vic, George Tabeek, and Lieutenant Andy Desperito opened the doors leading into the office spaces; George, using his master key on the locked doors, swept each floor for people. "Clear," each shouted when he determined no one was left.

Vic ran into a civilian with a large woman draped over his back at the same time firemen arrived. The firemen instructed the civilian that they would take care of her evacuation down the stairs.

"I'm Vic Guarnera with World Trade Security," Vic said, introducing himself to the civilian. "Would you please help us clear the floors?" he asked.

"I'm Sergeant Dennis Franklin, Port Authority Police," the "civilian" said, introducing himself to Vic. "Absolutely." They leapfrogged the floors down, clearing them to the main-lobby level, where the gate to the basement was locked as usual to prevent people from getting trapped in the sub-levels. Then they returned to the devastation of the main lobby.

###

10:04 A.M.

"Where is everyone?" Gabriella Ballini croaked, having raised her head out of the black, gritty water. It was as black as a Pennsylvania coal mine, and as quiet. "Where is everyone?" she repeated a little louder, expecting the worst, thinking she was the only person left alive.

"I'm here," a trembling, dislocated voice answered. "Here I am." It was a woman's voice . . . feeble, scared.

A hand flopped onto Gabriella's arm, found her hand, and grabbed it, holding tight. At the same moment, Gabriella's hearing returned. There was crying somewhere behind her, and screaming—people screaming for help. She recognized a voice straining through the darkness. It was the voice of a woman she knew from her office. Gabriella was coughing, spitting up that pasty, gritty substance that was everywhere. The sounds of coughing, screaming, and moaning were all around her. Moving her hands around, she felt glass and debris all over the travertine marble floor. She still had that old towel clutched in her hand and mopped her face.

Gabriella's mind was struggling to pull things together. She thought she knew where she was—near the escalator pit, behind the wall. Trying to get her bearings, she reached out and touched a wall. She was certain it was the escalator pit. *Thank God I didn't fall into that pit!* she exclaimed to herself. *So . . . that puts Duane Reade in that direction, north.*

In the faraway distance, Gabriella saw the beam of a flashlight, its faint shaft of light wagging back and forth. Others saw the light and there was a big commotion. In desperation, everyone struggled to walk or crawl toward that dim light. It represented hope, refuge, and a way out of this hellish, unfathomable nightmare.

The light slowly approached, a faint glimmer grappling to penetrate the thick, gritty smoke. A woman's hand had a tight grip on hers. No bones seemed to be broken and they both stood. The debris underfoot was dangerous. Dragging their feet through wires, broken walls, chunks of metal—sloshing through ankle-high water, crunching on glass—the going was treacherous and agonizingly slow. The shaft of light failed in its attempt to penetrate the thick, black atmosphere. It looked like a little doughnut, the solid airborne particles distorting the beam. When it reached Gabriella, she couldn't see who or what was holding it.

Gabriella felt like she was in front of the evacuation out of the mall. She was still holding hands with an unknown woman, and neither had spoken to the other. She slowly made her way toward the E-train platform—she thought, hoped. She really wasn't sure, but it felt like the right direction. There were a lot of people trying to follow her out. "I think the train is this way," Gabriella clumsily announced to the unknown woman whose hand she continued to hold. She didn't know, but was fairly certain that Vesey Street was also in that direction. The people were in a long procession behind her. There was not much talking; there was some murmuring and moaning from pain, but overall people were fairly calm. People were moving toward safety—they hoped.

The dust was beginning to thin. Here and there, Gabriella could see cables hanging from the ceiling, and the destruction of collapsed walls and broken plateglass windows. One agonizing step after another, still holding hands with a woman she didn't know, she continued making what she fervently hoped was progress. After what seemed an excruciatingly long time, she rounded a wall and heard voices ahead. And she saw what could only be faint daylight penetrating from above. The light came from the escalator in Five World Trade Center going up toward the Borders bookstore on Church Street.

10:05 A.M.

Andre Farkas, the Greenwich Board of Realtors' photographer, was driving into the garage as Sarah Ronningen drove toward the exit ramp. He noticed that Sarah was in distress and signaled her to stop. He pulled up alongside her, his window already rolled down. "Your husband, Erik, is down there, isn't he?" he asked, not expecting a reply to his rhetorical question.

"Yes," Sarah nodded, tears streaming down her cheeks, dripping off her chin.

"Do you know—?" He cut the question short.

Sarah shook her head from side to side, providing his answer.

"Will you be all right driving?" he inquired, concern in his voice.

"I'll be okay," she managed to get out. "I'm going to spend the day with my girlfriend Jackie. She's not far from here."

10:06 A.M.

It was pitch black, oily, wet, and difficult to breathe. Yvonne Barker's prayer had just been answered: "Form a human chain and come to the light. I'll get you out," a voice had instructed. Yvonne saw the light and tried to get up. She was so tired—exhausted. She had to get on all fours and literally pull herself up, limb by limb. At the time, she thought it was the most difficult act she had had to perform all day.

There was glass all over her clothing and body. She was soaking wet and the water had an oily texture. Her mouth felt like she had eaten a sand sandwich—like she and her friends used to joke as kids at the beach. *This is no day at the beach,* she reflected. Yvonne started to hobble, barefoot, toward the light and the man's voice.

A hand grabbed Yvonne's arm.

"Ahhh!" Yvonne screamed, startled, and turned in the direction of the hand's owner. It was a woman.

"You're hurt," the woman pronounced. She took the scarf from around her neck and wiped the blood off Yvonne's face.

Yvonne had lost her T-shirt, she realized with dismay—and, in horror, her evacuation companion, Flory.

"And you don't have any shoes on," the woman observed with concern and compassion. "Let's slow down," she suggested.

This woman must be one of God's angels, Yvonne thought. *How else could she know I don't have any shoes on?* It was dark and her bare feet were under even darker water.

"No. No. Please! I just want to get out of this building," Yvonne responded a bit harshly. "I just want to get out of this building. Don't slow down for me. I don't care."

Yvonne walked barefoot in the direction of the light. The closer she got the lighter it became in the mall. She began to see wires and metal and signs dangling out of the ceiling, and huge chunks of plate glass and metal all over the once highly polished terrazzo floor. All the store windows were broken, their interior displays a mess. "*This is a complete disaster,*" she concluded, and carefully put one aching foot in front of the other.

10:09 A.M.

For the first time, Jerry Dinkels thought there was a very real possibility that he was going to die in that absolute darkness. He couldn't breathe. He thought he was walking down into a burning inferno. There was no escape into cleaner air, because he'd tried the doors and they were locked. Jerry damned well didn't want to die. Certainly not like this! His thoughts turned to his wife, Mary Ellen.

"Do you want some oxygen?" a disembodied voice asked through the oily darkness.

Jerry forced his eyes open enough to recognize the shape of a fireman.

The fireman took his mask off and placed it firmly over Trish's mouth and nose. "Take a couple of deep breaths," he instructed Trish.

"Do you want some?" he asked, turning to Jerry.

"Ahhh . . ." Jerry croaked.

"Take it," the fireman said, putting the mask over Jerry's nose and mouth.

After two or three deep breaths of fresh oxygen, the fireman replaced his mask and disappeared, heading up into the tower. Jerry, with a new lease on life and Trish under his arm, made it down one more flight of stairs to the twenty-second floor.

Entering through the unlocked door into the core of the tower, Jerry noticed two colleagues he worked with on the Permanent Security Project, George Tabeek and Vic Guarnera. They were on the other side of the core helping people around what appeared to be a huge hole in the floor.

A fireman nearby told Jerry, "Go this way," and pointed to the B-stairwell.

"Is the stairwell clear?" Jerry asked, referring to the smoke.

"Yeah, it's clear enough."

"Is there anybody below to tell us what to do once we get there?"

"Yes," the fireman answered.

Jerry, with Trish under his wing, entered the B-stairwell and descended the remainder of the floors without incident. Stepping through the door into the B-corridor of the main lobby, Jerry was surprised to find that he was in ankle-deep water. Looking around through the haze, he was aghast!

Port Authority Police Officer David Lim stopped on the twenty-first floor. There were three other officers stopped on this floor. He wanted to confer, and get their assessment of the situation as his radio had recently stopped working.

"What's the situation?" Officer Lim asked.

"Tower Two has collapsed!" he was told, hastily.

"What! Say again?" he asked, requesting confirmation. David's hearing had been giving him trouble since the fireball exploded on the forty-fourth-floor sky lobby, and he wanted to be certain that he had heard correctly.

"Tower Two, the South Tower, has collapsed!" a second officer confirmed. "We've been given the order to evacuate this tower," he added.

Together, the four officers began running down the stairs. A couple floors down they picked up a couple more people who were hurt and helped them down. David saw a couple putting together a makeshift stretcher for another of the injured.

"There's no time for that," he yelled at the couple. "Just pick him up and carry him the best you can."

"Let's go! Let's go! Let's go!" There was a real sense of urgency in his voice, and people followed his command.

"Down is good!" David encouraged, exhausted, trying to husband his remaining energy. "Down is good!" he yelled, and the call was repeated up and down the winding stairs.

David had made it to the fifth-floor landing when he encountered a battalion chief and five other firefighters from Ladder Company 6 assisting a civilian, Josephine Harris.

"Hey, chief," Officer Lim offered. "Let me give you fellows a hand."

Josephine Harris was literally worn out. Her body shook from the long hike down from her seventy-third-floor office, and her legs no longer responded to the command to "keep walking down." And her bad feet were absolutely killing her.

"I've got to stop and rest," Josephine wheezed, exhausted, to her seven assisting attendants.

"You can do it, Josephine," they all encouraged in unison. "We've only a few flights left, and then we're out. Come on, one foot in front of the other. We'll help you. That-a-girl. You're doing great. We're almost there!"

They made it down two additional landings when Josephine announced, "Stop! I can't go another step!" She added, "You men go on without me. I'll be okay."

"We're not going anywhere without you, Josephine" they each said. "You're our girl and we all stick together. We're a team. Don't you worry."

Good to their word, they all rested with Josephine Harris on the fourth-floor landing of the North Tower.

The grit from that evil black cloud had collected in all of Erik Ronningen's pores. He couldn't breathe and truly thought that his time had come to go to his greater reward.

Erik was at his absolute end. Through sheer force of will he had commanded his body to keep walking east. The dark-gray vision began to get darker. He was light-headed, his lungs burned, and he felt his knees begin to buckle and his body collapse onto the street. At that same instant, he saw an even darker fuzzy movement slightly off to his right. Willing his last ounce of strength back into his buckling knees, he staggered toward the fuzzy movement, and followed a man into the kitchen door of a delicatessen.

The deli staff was handing out liquids. Erik took one life-giving gulp, washed the grit down his constricted throat—and was able to breathe again.

10:11 A.M.

Yvonne Barker dragged her battered, aching body out of the mall, up the steps, and out the doors onto Vesey Street. She felt relieved to be out of the buildings, but couldn't believe what she saw. Everyone was white! They were pasty white and walking around like zombies, nobody talking!

My eyes are ruined! she realized with horror. Everywhere she looked, she saw black and white. *Where is all the color?* she asked herself. The streets and sidewalks were ankle-deep in papers and thick, gray ash. The whole atmosphere was thick with a blizzard of falling ash. All the cars, ambulances, and fire trucks on Vesey Street were damaged. A cacophony of auto alarms filled the air. *We must be at war!* she concluded.

Yvonne looked like a zombie herself as she walked east on Vesey Street toward Church Street. She became aware of people running toward her, their clothes intact.

"How is it in there? Did you see any bodies?" Microphones were thrust in her face, and she saw bright floodlights and cameras filming her.

Reporters! she deduced.

"Did you see lots of dead people? Did you see any blood?" The questions continued, the lights blinding. "How about burned people?"

All her life, Yvonne had detested the insensitivity of reporters. During tragic events, they took advantage of people in their weakest moments—moments when the victims should be left alone to find themselves, to come to grips with what they have just experienced. And here they were with all their insensitivity, asking her the same thoughtless questions.

"Did you see any blood?" one reporter repeated anxiously.

"I'll show you blood!" Yvonne erupted.

For an hour and a half, Yvonne had been escaping from one horror after another in her efforts to evade death at the hands of the World Trade Center towers. She had survived the first horrible shaking and eruptions, and the sudden, huge hole through the floors blocking the escape from her office. She had made it through the black, smoky tower core into the crowded stairwells. She had negotiated the smoke-filled stairs, past civilians putting out fires. And just when she thought she was safe, the mall had turned into Satan's carnival. And now this! Her body was shaking badly from exhaustion, she had lost her color vision, she was wet and pasty-white, the city looked like it had been bombed and the people like zombies, she was standing in ash up to her ankles, she was worried about her family . . . and now these damned, perfectly attired reporters were asking her insensitive questions! She had reached the end of her self-control, patience, composure, and decorum. *Damn them all!*

"I'll show you blood!" Yvonne exploded again, lifting her ankle-length skirt high above her head, any remaining glass flinging off. And there she was for all the world to see, with a long, deep gash in her right knee, blood leaking out, streaming down her leg, collecting on her bare right foot.

Yvonne was the very picture of disaster, tragedy, and catastrophe all wrapped into one. Without a word she dropped her skirt, and in total disgust and disdain, stomped off into the smoky haze of war.

At Church Street she turned left, walking north. She only knew it was Church Street because through the thick haze she recognized the post office, an imposing government structure that served the World Trade Center complex. An ambulance was parked nearby and an attendant ran over to her.

"You're hurt," he announced. "Come here. Come to us; we'll fix you up."

Yvonne looked back over her left shoulder and saw the fires in World Trade Center Building Five, and in the top of Tower One.

"No," she replied, worn out. "I just want to go home. I'm okay." Yvonne didn't know what had happened; she just knew that she wanted to get away. Nor did she know the seriousness of her wound. As she continued to walk north, she stopped at one ambulance after another to ask for a Band-Aid. She knew they were all treating the real casualties, but she still couldn't believe it. Not one ambulance had a Band-Aid! One EMT gave her a piece of gauze and told her to "press and walk." "Treat and street" was the EMT slang for it; treat 'em, move 'em out, treat the next one. So she pressed and walked.

"Oh, sister, you're hurt!" a man talking on his cell phone shouted, looking up at Yvonne and hanging up.

"I'm okay. I'm okay."

"No!" he countered. "Hell no! You're not okay! I'm going to find somebody to help you."

"No, really," she retorted. "All I need is a Band-Aid."

Yelling over his shoulder to stay where she was, the man ran and brought back an ambulance attendant.

"Show me your injury," the attendant commanded.

"I just need a Band-Aid," she said, picking up her skirt, exposing her wounded right knee and bloodied leg. "I just want to go home."

"You need more than a Band-Aid!" the man who came to her rescue said. "Get into the ambulance," he commanded.

10:13 A.M.

Gabriella Ballini could now see, and there was glass and debris everywhere. And chaos! Everyone else in the decimated mall had seen the light, and the way out. The self-organized group of a moment ago instantly turned into a free-for-all. Gabriella became separated from her unknown companion escapee, and jogged up the escalator, closely followed by everyone behind her. Jogging, kicking through chunks of glass, she ran straight through what were once a huge plateglass window-wall and revolving doors, out onto Church Street.

It's nuclear war! Gabriella immediately thought upon getting outdoors. Her mind felt partially paralyzed. The realization hit her with the force of a ten-megaton bomb. "It's nuclear war! My family is dead!" She moaned to herself.

It was a blizzard of gray fallout. An empty desert—and the biggest blizzard she had ever seen, or could even imagine! A total whiteout! The fallout was ankle deep and continued to rain down. Everyone was panicking and running. A firefighter nearby was yelling, "Run! Run!" The fallout was so thick Gabriella could hardly breathe. She pushed that soggy, filthy towel in front of her face, but it didn't help. All she could think of was her family—all dead. This was a war. She knew it. She couldn't see. The grit was accumulating in her eyes, grinding under her contacts. She started running up what must have been Fulton Street. She couldn't see the buildings and veered left at Broadway, ending up on Park Row at J&Rs, the big electronics store. The nuclear blizzard continued with unabated fervor. There was no color in the world—only gray. And so thick! Breathing was impossible. Gabriella saw people behind glass doors, hiding out in stores to escape the fallout.

She saw Harriett Donaldson, the first person she knew that survived. They approached each other and hugged, saying nothing, just mumbling incoherently. Harriett looked totally dazed. She must have looked the way Gabriella felt: dazed, exhausted, and confused.

A bus stopped and somebody yelled, "Get on the bus!" Gabriella got on with everyone else, but the bus didn't move. Someone handed out bottled water. No one said anything, but there was crying, and coughing. Eventually the bus lurched forward. It drove three blocks north and let everyone off at City Hall.

Gabriella didn't know where the rest of the people in downtown New York went, but they were—gone! It didn't matter.

"I'm alive! I'm alive!" That's what mattered.

"Now, for my family . . ."

10:16 A.M.

At the bottom of the stairwell, Tad Hanc came to an open door, and stepping through it, he sensed that he was in a large open area. The dust was so thick and black he couldn't see anything, but had the feeling they had reached the concourse level, one level above the main lobby of Tower One.

Those huge, huge windows overlooking the plaza, which normally let in so much light, today allowed in only darkness. And he could barely breathe. Somewhere he had lost his undershirt that he'd wrapped around his face, and he was breathing in thick grit. Tad flashed his light around trying to attract someone's attention. Someone far away flashed a light in his direction. "Which way do I get out?" he yelled at the light.

"Go this way," the light pointed. "Come this way," the faraway voice shouted.

Dragging his feet through the debris, gasping for air, Tad noticed two girls nearby. They were shouting and crying, not moving, so Tad walked over to them. "Grab my hands," he instructed, taking theirs, and dragged them toward the flashing light. When they reached the person with the light, they were told to go through the broken window and walk under the overhang of Six World Trade Center, the Customs House.

"Don't look up! Don't look up!" the man with the light shouted. "Just go around to that overhang."

10:21 A.M.

Tad Hanc had seen the airplane as it nearly flew into his office. Despite the warnings not to do so, Tad now looked up and saw flames coming out of the tower. And debris. Staggering toward the overhang of the Customs House, he heard what sounded like a shotgun going off right in front of him. He stumbled over something soft and lumpy, regained his balance, and kept on walking. He looked around and couldn't believe what he saw. Stuff was falling out of the tower, and the plaza was covered in debris, metal, and other things.

What happened to the trees? Tad thought. *All the leaves are gone, and what is all that stuff hanging off the branches?* It looked like winter, or nuclear winter; the fallout was so thick he could hardly walk through it. *Where did everyone go?* Tad wondered. He became aware that he was all alone in this eerie, gray, nightmarish wilderness. Tad thought he had lost most of his vision. He could barely see, the two girls were gone, the people he was with in the stairwell . . . disappeared. Looking south to Tower Two, he couldn't see farther than ten feet ahead of him. Tad was in the thickest, darkest cloud of fog he'd ever been in. Stuff continued to rain down on him. He heard loud crashing sounds, and what sounded like shotguns discharging behind him. Slowly he waded through the wreckage, past the day care center, toward the stairs and escalator going down to Vesey Street on the north side of the Trade Center.

"What is that noise?" Tad mumbled to himself. He could hear dozens and dozens of what sounded like little car alarms. He heard the sounds of alarms from all around. His vision slowly returning, he looked around and noticed lots of cars, some ambulances, police cars, and a fire truck— all damaged, and all with their alarms going off.

Trudging east on Vesey, going toward Church Street, Tad looked up and saw that Five World Trade Center was on fire. The roof was on fire and flames were coming out of the windows.

From out of the smoke, haze, and fog, a man materialized and asked, "Sir, are you injured?"

"Why? Why?" Tad asked, not understanding the cause for the question.

"You're all covered with blood!" the man exclaimed.

For the first time, Tad looked down at himself and saw that he was covered in blood. Using his hands to feel himself, checking for cuts, he seemed to be okay.

"No, I'm fine," Tad reported. "I don't know what happened. This isn't my blood," and he turned left onto Church Street, walking north.

"Excuse me," a woman said, thrusting a microphone in Tad's face. "Could you tell us what happened? You're injured!" she said, astonished. "What happened?"

"No. No. I have no time for this," Tad said impatiently. "I have to go to FBI headquarters. I have this story to tell them." Looking around through the thick haze, not seeing anyone, thinking he was the only one to survive, Tad asked her, "Do you know where all the people are?" Tad was coming to the stark, terrible realization that perhaps he was the only one to make it out of the towers alive.

She looked at him like he was a little crazy, took a step backward shaking her head, and walked away, disappearing into the fog and leaving him all alone to figure things out for himself.

Tad walked two blocks north on Church Street, but it was so thick with debris and ash he made the decision to turn left at Park Place and walk west toward the Hudson River—two blocks north of Tower One.

Vic Guarnera and Sergeant Dennis Franklin, PAPD, exited the B-stairwell into the main lobby. It was in complete and total shambles. And everything was gray. There was no color anywhere. Nor were there any civilians; only uniformed police and firemen remained. Walking toward the Fire Command Desk in the northwest corner of the main lobby, Vic said to the firemen, "You fellows need to get out of the tower right now!" But as he expected, his orders fell on deaf ears.

Planning to leave by the North Bridge to the World Financial Center, Vic looked outdoors and was shocked at the amount of rubble and wreckage. The world outdoors, looking through broken windows, was a field of gray debris with lumps of gray carelessly strewn about. He and Dennis walked up the escalator to the North Bridge, but before crossing, Vic said, "Naw. We don't want to go over the bridge." *If someone hits the bridge we'll be exposed and the bridge will collapse onto West Street with us on it*, Vic reasoned to himself.

Turning to Dennis he instructed, "Okay. Let's go out this way." And they waded through the debris and ankle-high dust around the perimeter of the Customs Building, Six World Trade Center, and through the paper and junk down the escalator by the day care center to Vesey Street. They were both exhausted, and Vic, still in evacuation mode and now out of the tower, was not aware of the horrific cause and extent of the damage.

Dragging their exhausted bodies west on Vesey toward West Street, Sergeant Dennis Franklin turned to Vic and said, "Vic, I want you to make me a promise."

"Okay."

"If you get out of here and I don't, I want you to make sure that this watch gets to my kids," he said, extending his left arm and showing Vic the watch on his wrist.

"Okay," Vic repeated.

"No! I'm serious," Dennis said. "Look at this," he insisted, thrusting his wrist toward Vic's face. "This is a Rolex! This is an $8,000 watch! I don't want my ex to get it! Make sure that my kids get it."

"Dennis, you're on! It's not a problem. I'll make you that promise."

They arrived at the FDNY command post at Vesey and West Streets, and Vic tried using the same logic that he had used on Lieutenant Andy Desperito on FDNY Deputy Chief Flaherty: "Chief, you've got to move the command post and all your equipment west or north, away from the tower." As he was talking, Vic heard that sound—the same awful, gut-wrenching sound he heard twenty-nine minutes ago, the same cannon-like, thunderous snap he heard when the top of the South Tower fell off.

10:23 A.M.

Jerry Dinkels and Trish Cullen finally exited the B-corridor stairwell, stepping into ankle-deep water in the main lobby "What!" Jerry exclaimed, refusing to believe what he was seeing. He was astounded by the state of the security project he had worked on—the bright, shiny, custom-made turnstiles were all caked with dirt. The marble walls were cracked and in broken piles on the floor.

What happened here? he asked himself. Jerry knew something had happened high in the tower, but he couldn't fathom what might have caused the devastation he was seeing down in the lobby. *The lobby is decimated!* he thought.

"Come this way," a voice directed, coming from the west side of the lobby. It was a policeman. "Be careful," he cautioned as he helped them through the broken plateglass windows, directing them to West Street. "Don't look back. Just keep walking north," he instructed.

What Jerry saw chilled his blood. There was metal, glass, pieces of furniture, tons of paper, debris . . . and . . . and . . . Jerry had to blink his stinging eyes, squeezing them shut and opening them again. He realized that he indeed saw what he thought he was seeing—bodies! Dead bodies scattered like confetti.

Forcing himself to keep walking and looking around, he saw lots of emergency vehicles with their lights flashing—but no people! He turned, walking north on West Street. Looking up at the North Bridge—the covered pedestrian bridge connecting the World Trade Center with the World Financial Center west of West Street—Jerry noticed that all the windows of the bridge were broken, like they had been blown out.

"Oh, God!" Jerry exclaimed. "Somebody must have gotten killed there!" He walked under the bridge, reached Vesey Street, stopped, and turned around to look back in the direction from which he had just come, when a new horror confronted him.

"Two's gone?" Jerry asked himself aloud, puzzled. Pausing, staring into the smoke and dirt cloud, he came to the awful conclusion. "Achille!" Jerry pronounced, "Two's gone!"

"No. No," Achille contradicted, studying what looked like the field of battle. "It's just the smoke and the angle."

"No! No!" Jerry insisted. "Two is gone!"

"Oh, my God!" Achille shouted, like the realization of having put his hand on a hot stove, quickly jerking it off. "It's like somebody ripped the face of the earth off."

Jerry began walking north again, looking back over his shoulder. Looking high up at the North Tower, he saw that it was burning. Flames and smoke were shooting out of the top floors. And every so often a cluster of dark objects would fall from the windows—people jumping, arms and legs flailing, tumbling, falling to the sidewalk. Each time there was a jumper, the crowd would groan in unison, feeling the agony and pain of their friends and colleagues, privately thanking God that it was not them. The sight of those poor jumpers—Jerry would remember that the rest of his life.

As Jerry turned to continue walking north, glancing up at the 347-foot-high broadcast antenna atop the North Tower, he heard Achille pronounce, "At least the bastards didn't get the antenna!" The antenna provided a significant source of income from all the radio and television broadcasters.

At that precise moment, the antenna began to condense.

10:25 A.M.

Captain Anthony Whitaker had cleaned himself up as best as he could, splashing water on his face after being caught in the dust from the collapse. He had returned to the command center on West Street, where he ran into Alan Reiss, the director of the World Trade Department before Larry Silverstein Properties had taken over six week ago. Looking up at the remaining tower, Tony asked Alan, "Do you think it will fall?"

"It is going to fall," Alan stated matter-of-factly, as calmly as if he were asking for the salt to sprinkle on his French fries.

The way Alan stated that the tower was going to collapse, and the look on his face when he said it, convinced Tony that the North Tower was going to collapse any minute. Tony immediately ran over to the Port Authority Police command bus and instructed the driver to head north up West Street. The bus was blocked by fire trucks, so Tony went to each one and told the drivers, "Get out of here! The building is coming down!"

As the fire trucks began moving north toward Chambers Street, everyone began running. When they got about a block away there was the sound of a tremendous crack, and a volcanic explosion.

###

10:27 A.M.

Tad Hanc, covered in others' blood, reached West Broadway and saw a crate of bottled water sitting on the sidewalk. *I am really thirsty*, he realized. He'd been entirely focused on getting out, safely away from the burning tower, falling debris, and thick cloud of dirt and grit. However, seeing the bottled water, he suddenly became aware of how terribly parched he was. Walking toward the crate, Tad saw Tom Rabazinsky, someone he knew from the engineering department and the only other person besides himself that Tad thought had made it out alive.

"Tom, Tom!" Tad called. "Why don't you have a drink of water with me?" But either Tom didn't hear his invitation or was in a state of shock, as he ignored Tad's offer and wandered away.

Tad reached down and pulled a bottle out of the crate. As he stood up, twisting the cap off and throwing his head back to take a deep swig, looking up Tad saw the flaming inferno that was the top of Tower One.

###

10:28 A.M.

In mid-guzzle, watching Tower One in flames, all of a sudden Tad Hanc saw the upper building that was above the fire zone begin to collapse. "Oh, my God!" Tad blurted, the water spraying out of his mouth. And he knew that the tower was coming down.

Survival reflexes automatically kicked in and Tad found himself running, rounding a corner to put some buildings between him and the collapsing tower. Tad was only two blocks north of Tower One, and he didn't need to be an engineer to know that the 1,368-foot-high tower could easily engulf many square blocks, one of which he was occupying. Running, Tad saw his friend Tom running in the same direction, but lost him when he thought he saw him duck into a doorframe of a building for protection. When he reached the middle of the block, on a side street of buildings, Tad stopped to wait . . . to see what happened.

The noise was terrifying! And all the debris and smoke was going uptown. Tad couldn't believe it. The tower had missed him, and he just stood right there in the middle of the street as the dust cloud billowed north on both streets to either side of him. He was untouched by debris and cloud!

"I'm still alive!" he exclaimed, hardly believing his good fortune.

Eventually, Tad continued walking west, toward the Hudson River. When he got to West Street, he turned north. People were standing around the streets looking south, watching. So Tad decided to stop and see for himself what all the interest was.

Turning around to look south he had a clear view of the towers—except he couldn't see them. He saw only a huge pile of debris and steel, fire, smoke, and dust. And looking—and looking some more—the full and complete realization of what had happened, where he had been, and what he had just escaped enveloped him in a paradox of mournful, heavyhearted, and joyous relief. Tad Hanc sank to the curb, broke down, and cried like a baby.

Achille Niro had just pronounced to Jerry Dinkels that the bastards hadn't destroyed the antenna—when at that moment the antenna began to shrink.

One second later, Jerry Dinkels heard the deafening, thunderous crash of the collapsing North Tower. Instantly, Jerry began running as fast as his legs would propel him away from the increasing danger. Stampeding with the throng, Jerry saw firemen hightailing it north, struggling out of their Scott packs, throwing them aside, and removing their masks and turnout gear.

Jerry didn't think he had much fight left in him, but when he looked down at the pavement and saw a dark shadow overtaking him, blotting out the sun, he dug deep down to the bottom of his toes and found the strength to continue pounding his size-8½ feet northward. Trish was still tethered to him, and Achille was running with a woman a little to his rear.

The dark, silent, black shadow very quickly overtook them all.

I hope nothing big hits me, Jerry thought with a calmness he didn't think he had in him, all the while pounding one foot in front of the other through the darkening day. He knew Chambers Street was just ahead. On the left was Stuyvesant High School. The decision was a no-brainer as he made a quick turn and entered the school lobby with Trish on his arm.

Just as they entered and shut the door, they heard a "swoosh!" as the smoke and black cloud, carrying the pulverized contents and remains of the North Tower, blew past them—and the world turned dark.

###

West Street was packed with equipment: fire apparatus, emergency personnel vehicles, ambulances, response trucks—you name it, it was all there. Vic Guarnera was attempting to convince FDNY Deputy Chief Flaherty to move his command post and all his equipment away from the North Tower when he heard another explosion. *The second bomb,* he thought. "Let's get the hell out of here!" Vic yelled, and off he ran, north up West Street.

There was a thunderous roar, like the sound of a thousand locomotives under a thousand-car load. It was like standing under a 747 taking off—so loud it was deafening—and the earth shook so recklessly he could hardly stand. Vic commanded his sixty-seven-year-old legs to keep moving, but then that black, evil cloud threw itself over him, plunging him into total darkness. The cloud was thick; it was like breathing through sand, so Vic pulled his jacket up and over his face and mouth, trying to breathe. Small pieces of the tower were pelting his body, and as he ran smack into a piece of fire equipment, something slammed into the back of his right leg, and his legs began to buckle. *I'm not going down. I am not going down,* he thought to himself over and over. He was determined not to be a casualty, and he recovered, stayed on his feet, and kept moving. He couldn't see anything in the black, sandstorm darkness, nor could he breathe as he felt his way around the fire truck he had run into. He cautiously kept moving north, knowing he was going to run into another piece of equipment.

Time stopped for Vic as he tried to deal with what could be the end of the world. Nothing in all his training had prepared him for this: the deafening sound of the collapse, the pitch-blackness of that sand-filled cloud, the inferno of heat and wind, the pressure compressing every square inch of his body. It was like something right out of Dante.

Then the blackness began to brighten, and looking about, Vic puzzled out that he had somehow struggled half a block north toward Barclay Street. He continued walking. With each block of progress north, the day continued to brighten and the debris-strewn street began to thin out. Ever the first responder, he immediately began looking for the command post. He wanted to help because he knew there were going to be people trapped in the basements of the tower, and he knew the towers like the back of his hand. Off to his left was Stuyvesant High School, his alma mater, from which he had graduated fifty years ago. Lots of people were going in and out of the school, so in he dragged himself.

"Who is the incident commander here?" Vic asked a group of people. "Where is the command post?" And someone pointed him toward the principal's office.

###

Captain Anthony Whitaker, a block north on West Street, turned when he heard the volcanic explosion and watched as the antenna on the top of Tower One began to slide into the building. He yelled to Alan Reiss, "It's coming down! Let's go!" Tony and Alan were running side by side along with the rest of the panicking crowd. They both looked back and saw that black, evil cloud begin to form and charge up West Street. At around Chambers Street they both knew they could not outrun that cloud.

"We're not going to make it!" Tony panted to Alan. And together they dived behind a curb with a steel guard. When the evil onslaught had passed, they got up and struggled to the police command bus and stumbled inside to try to escape the remainder of the clogging, gritty dust cloud. Tony directed the driver to the Borough of Manhattan Community

College at Chambers Street, where a sergeant of the New York City Police Department promptly informed them that car bombs were exploding.

Tony could hear explosions everywhere around him. Everyone began panicking again and there was mass hysteria.

The community college became their base of operations until, at Tony's request, they re-established the command center in an unused building at Four Vesey Street.

The ambulance attendant could see that Yvonne Barker's leg needed stitches and he commanded her to get into the ambulance. She got into it reluctantly. *All these people are really hurt; nobody needs to attend to me,* she thought. *They are pasty-white, just like me, and bleeding. I'm going to be sitting here forever. I just want to go home.* Her sights were on the Brooklyn Bridge. All she wanted to do was get to the bridge and walk across. She would be home soon.

Suddenly, it was déjà vu all over again. Everyone everywhere began screaming and running. Legs and arms pumping, looking over their shoulders, panic-stricken, people were running up Church Street as if a great tsunami was about to engulf them all.

"Oh, God! Not again!" Yvonne yelled as she scrambled to get out of the ambulance. She was desperate, panic-stricken. *I can't take this anymore,* she told herself. *I can't run another step.* Just as she was about to make her escape, someone dragged her back into the ambulance. The attendant locked the doors from the outside, ran around, and jumped into the driver's seat—and screamed!

"The tower is falling. Oh, God!" he screamed. Gunning the engine, he made a hasty U-turn and sped north up Church Street.

In the B-stairwell, on the fourth-floor landing of Tower One, Port Authority Police Officer David Lim and the six firefighters from Ladder Company 6 refused to leave Josephine Harris. Panic was rapidly about to gain the upper hand, as their progress out of the tower had come to a standstill.

At that same instant, the lights went out. Each man's private, unspoken worst fears became dreaded reality. They knew the fate of the South Tower. They had been given the order to evacuate the North Tower. They feared the imminent fate of the North Tower—their lives had just come to an end.

Instantaneously, the unbearable air pressure compressed every molecule of their bodies. Their closed eyes felt as though a champion wrestler's thumbs had pushed the orbs to the back of their skulls; the mother of all avalanches dumped tens of thousands of tons of concrete, steel, marble, and glass down around them, sucking at their clothing, attempting to drag them into the maelstrom to make them one with the catastrophe. The sound! It immediately deafened them, but still they could hear through their skin, feel the ten thousand high-speed freight trains colliding in a tunnel. Their lives were in the hands of their Maker as they shook and vibrated like they were in the Devil's rock crusher being turned into gravel.

On and on the never-ending nightmare continued. The noise was like being inside the Police Explosive Unit's detonation truck—during detonation. The impossible pressure was like free-diving to one hundred feet; the vibration pulverized the brain; the heat . . . it was like the heat of a pizza oven.

Gripping, gripping, gripping, eyes squeezed shut, teeth clenched. It was like a childhood nightmare of an endless carnival ride—knowing your life was at an end as you slipped into the exposed, revolving gears, screaming to stop the ride, watching all the laughing faces as you slid closer and closer toward the open gear box. It was the ultimate nightmare come to fruition.

The instant the lights went out—in the ten seconds that became an eternity—it was over.

Officer David Lim couldn't hear anything. The tornado of wind had violently thrown him head over heels. There was no sound—only deafening silence. He didn't know if he was in a dream. He wasn't quite certain what had just happened. He remembered that he was in trouble . . . and then it began to come back to him, in all the terrible reality. It was black where he was, wherever he was. He noticed that he wasn't breathing and couldn't figure out why. He couldn't see; he couldn't hear. Nobody could survive what he thought had just happened. That being said, it dawned on him what his condition was.

He was dead.

It was that simple. And he wasn't afraid.

He looked up and saw the faintest spot of light high above him and knew it must be the archangel Gabriel, come to take him from hell to heaven.

"Ohhhhh...."

Moaning sounds? Officer Lim questioned, surprised. *What's going on?*

He was coated in inches of muck, and had to dig it out of his eyes and mouth in order to breathe. "Hello?" he finally ventured, taking a hesitant sample breath. The air was not good, but breathable if you didn't mind inhaling thick dirt. "Are you guys there?" he asked cautiously.

One by one, the little rescue team checked in, as did their charge, Josephine Harris. Slowly, each began to feel about his body, checking for damage, making little comments to assure the others that he was okay. They were brothers, and brothers looked after one another. *Are we not our brother's keeper?* It appeared that the group had escaped—absent minor bumps and bruises, and perhaps a broken bone and maybe a mild concussion—major incident and death.

If ever there was a miracle, this would be one for the books, David thought.

Officer David Lim looked up again through the thick, palpable darkness. He saw that the dim light was still there, but now knew that it was not the archangel Gabriel. Thinking it was a light fixture that had escaped destruction, David wanted to investigate. Left hand on the stair rail he carefully stood and began to climb. It was dark, so he felt each stair with his foot, testing its stability before advancing to the next step. Looking up, he confirmed that the dim light was still there.

What is that? he wondered. One careful step at a time, David eventually made it up four flights—two floors—when the steps abruptly ended! He was as high as he could go, except the light fixture was still dimly lit far above him.

How could that be? he questioned. Curious, he stood there; hand on the railing to maintain his balance, David tilted his head back and just watched that little light.

Watching, watching, he became aware that the light was slowly starting to get a little brighter. Mesmerized by this strange phenomenon,

David couldn't take his eyes off that light. It continued to get brighter and brighter.

Suddenly, with a dawning of realization, David was alternately mystified and thrilled, puzzled and delighted, confused and enlightened. The light continued to brighten with an intensity, the only explanation of which was that it was—the sun!

"It's the sun!" he shouted.

Port Authority Police Officer David Lim was standing on top of what remained of the North Tower, Tower One of the World Trade Center.

10:45 A.M.

Nancy Seliga and Bob Benacchio, camouflaged in gray fallout, had trudged through Battery Park and up the east side toward the South Street Seaport.

"Can you believe it!?" a man shouted, leaning out of his apartment window when he saw Nancy and Bob scuffle by. "The damned towers fell!" They were somewhere around Peck Slip, just beyond the South Street Seaport Museum.

"Yeah, right!" they both said. They turned, looked at each other, and just kept walking. Nancy and Bob were in charge of Tower One. They both ran the towers and knew better than anyone that those buildings would be operational halfway through the next millennium.

Nancy and Bob discovered that they had walked to Chinatown, picking up friends and coworkers along the way. When they got to Chatham Square they both turned around to look back at their towers to see if the fires were out.

The towers were gone! All they could see was thick smoke hovering over where the towers should have been.

That man yelling from the apartment window had been right.

With tears welling up in their eyes, they hugged—long and hard. They had grown up together in the Port Authority family. They were like brother and sister, and they had just lost their home.

EPILOGUES

Gabriella Ballini

Walking north, it was obvious to everyone evacuating lower Manhattan that Gabriella Ballini had been in the collapse. She looked a mess, like she'd survived the rigors inside a rotating concrete mixer. She was inundated with cell phones—such was the overwhelming generosity of New Yorkers to her obvious plight. After the fifth or sixth offer, Gabriella finally got through to her husband, Neil.

"Tell everybody I'm alive!" she shouted into the phone. She was blubbering all over herself, crying from happiness or relief. "Call my mother—!" she instructed just as the connection was lost. Gabriella handed the phone back and began jogging toward the Hudson River.

When she reached the New York Ferry terminal on Forty-Second Street, Gabriella clambered onboard a ferry with a thousand other people. They all got off in Hoboken, New Jersey, and she took the PATH train to Newark Penn Station, where she transferred to New Jersey Transit.

When she got off at her station, it was obvious to everyone around her where she had been that morning. People offered to drive her home. She accepted and arrived to the open, welcoming arms of her handsome and loving husband, Neil, and their three young children—and a household of well-wishers.

Sonia Henriquez

After Sonia Henriquez had run several blocks east on Fulton Street, she stopped, reached into her backpack, and pulled out her cell phone. She called her best friend, Nell, another Port Authority employee who worked on the sixty-third floor of Tower One. There was no answer. So she called Nell's husband who had an office on Fulton Street near the Strand Book Store Annex. His answering machine greeted her.

"Jim, I'm okay, but I don't know about Nell," Sonia said into the machine. "Is she okay? I'm out of the building. I'm out of the building. But I don't know about Nell. Call me!" And she severed the connection.

Sonia was on Nassau Street when the second plane flew into the South Tower. She didn't see it, but when she heard the tremendous explosion, she thought the North Tower had exploded, killing everyone. She was beside herself, crying, sobbing, weeping. She knew that all her friends, including her best friend, Nell, were dead.

"Sonia! Sonia!" she heard a man's voice call out. She turned and it was a coworker. They walked farther north on Nassau Street and got a clear view of the towers. Much to Sonia's relief, Tower One had not fallen. But she could see the hole in the north face, and when bodies began falling, and people on the street corner started to keep count, it was more than she could endure.

"Oh, my God!" they chanted together. "There's another one! And another just jumped! Oh, my God!"

Sonia had family in Brooklyn and, with the tens of thousands of other people evacuating lower Manhattan, she walked over the Manhattan Bridge. She called a friend to pick her up to take her to her cousin's home. Sonia was exhausted, sweaty, and a little bloodied from a fall in the ordeal, and when she arrived, all her relatives were there and they had a big reunion.

Looking back, Sonia knows that God saved her life that fateful morning when He told her to go get a cup of coffee. To this day, her daily ritual is to get a cup of coffee every morning before she gets into the office.

Sonia now works in the general manager's office at LaGuardia Airport.

Jerrold M. Dinkels

Jerry Dinkels and Trish Cullen walked north on West Street—after Jerry found Trish a pair of boots several sizes too large for her, to replace the shoes she'd lost somewhere in the evacuation—and rejoined some of the folks with whom they'd evacuated. The crowd was panicked by a few scares of poison gas, gas leaks, and car bombs, especially when police and fire trucks sped north with sirens and lights flashing.

At Fourteenth Street, after being interviewed by CNN, Trish left to join some of her relatives at a friend's house. Jerry continued walking to the Chelsea Piers and took a cruise liner over to Hoboken, New Jersey. He walked to the Port Authority Technical Center in Jersey City, eventually making his way to the Journal Square Building where an emergency operations center (EOC) was quickly set up—since the center in the World Trade Center no longer existed. Sometime that afternoon, Jerry got word to his wife, Mary Ellen, that he was okay. He worked the telephones at the EOC for nearly forty-eight hours straight, unable to sleep in the cot provided, before going home on Thursday.

Jerry and his seven associates were awarded the Civilian Commendation Award for Bravery, Heroism, and Valor by the Port Authority for their heroic contribution to the elevator rescue.

After eighteen years, the last four spent working at the Port Authority Technical Center in Jersey City, New Jersey, on August 31, 2005, Jerry Dinkels retired from the Port Authority of New York and New Jersey.

Edward Bonny

Ed Bonny made it through the remaining horror of the day at the Port Authority Technical Center in Jersey City. He fielded phone calls, and put together lists of known survivors . . . and the missing.

When the North Tower collapsed, Ed had a "heart feeling" that his wife, Pat, was okay. He did not have definitive knowledge of her safety until later that afternoon, when his thirteen-year-old daughter, Danielle, answered the family telephone and spoke to her mother calling from a midtown restaurant. Pat had evacuated, walking through the carnage of the plaza, and was about four blocks northeast when the North Tower collapsed, escaping the black cloud. As Ed predicted, at 8:30 that evening she returned safely home.

Ed Bonny is the last person to have seen John Fisher alive as he strode purposefully into the lobby of Tower One at 8:53 a.m. John reached the Operations Command Center in the B-1 basement level of the South Tower and, with Doug Karpiloff, is credited for saving thousands of lives, assisting in the evacuation of employees from the towers.

Ed and Pat continue to work for the Port Authority of New York and New Jersey. They reside in New Jersey with their daughter, Danielle. For many years, their home overlooked the scarred sight of where the Twin

Towers of the World Trade Center once stood. And in recent years they have been privileged to watch the Phoenix rise—the erection of World Trade Center Tower Seven, and lately, World Trade Center Tower One, formerly known as the Freedom Tower.

Jim Usher

Jim Usher made it safely to a nearby hospital. He sat patiently for many hours as a doctor extracted from his skin thousands of minute shards of Tower Two's plate-glass windows, pulverized from the explosion of the seventy-seventh to eighty-fifth floors.

Jim spent the night in the city. Late the next morning he walked over to the west side of Manhattan and got on the ferry to Hoboken. Once in Hoboken he boarded a train to Glen Rock, NJ where his eldest daughter Karen met him and drove him home to start the healing process. After six months recuperating, healing both mentally and physically, Jim formed his own technology consulting business and has grown it into a successful enterprise.

As a memento of his 9/11-survival experience, Jim framed and mounted his "I want my daughters to know the cause of my death" photograph above the fireplace mantel of his country home. And centered on the mantelpiece under the photograph, sealed inside a five-inch-high crystal cylinder, are the two thousand-plus minute shards of glass that were tweezered from his body. The little bronze metal plaque Jim had custom made and affixed to its base reads: September 11, 2001. And centered under it the number: 2,749.

Of the many miracles from that day, Jim Usher has no visible scarring . . . and he continues to put the Marlboro Man to shame.

Mike Craparo

When Mike crossed the North Bridge and reached the World Financial Center, he was certain that there had been an earthquake. Mike fully intended to help set up a command center, but he noticed that the FDNY and NYPD had already established centers on West Street just slightly north of Vesey. After accounting for his fifteen visitor greeters and assuring their safety, instructing them to find a way home, Mike also began making his way home to his wife, Terri.

Mike had been in law enforcement most of his life, and knew the chaos created when "volunteers" volunteered to insert themselves into the already well-established structure of commands. Though he knew he would not be turned away, he also knew he would be more a hindrance than a help, as hundreds of first responders were on the scene doing what first responders do. Reluctantly, yet knowing he was taking the right course of action, he found his way home to the welcoming arms of his wife.

Mike is currently head of security at a prestigious museum in uptown Manhattan.

Yvonne R. Barker

Yvonne was driven to Beth Israel Hospital on First Avenue and Sixteenth Street, where a plastic surgeon treated the wounds on her right knee with forty stitches. While she was in recovery she managed to get a telephone call through to her boyfriend. When he answered and heard Yvonne's voice, he began crying hysterically. "My God! You're alive!" he yelled.

Get a grip! Yvonne thought.

Later that afternoon, a friend picked Yvonne up from Beth Israel and brought her to her home near the United Nations. It was only when she began to watch the television coverage that she saw the magnitude of what she had just escaped. Crying, she telephoned her boyfriend to apologize; she didn't know what the world had been watching.

After six months on convalescent leave, Yvonne returned to work three days a week. Her boss and evacuation partner, Flory Danish, returned twelve months later.

Nearing the first anniversary of 9/11, she received a telephone call from the New York Police Department. "We've found some of your belongings from the World Trade Center," the officer told her. "Would you like to come down and claim them?" he asked. In the sixteen acres of concrete, steel, pulverized debris, and burned-out rubble, they had found a perfectly preserved photograph of Yvonne's granddaughter.

"Imagine that!" she said, astonished. "Paper! A piece of paper from my desk on the eighty-sixth floor!"

She missed the wedding of her best friend's son on the beach in Saint Martin. There would be other weddings, and other beaches.

Yvonne has retired on full pension from the Port Authority of New York and New Jersey.

Captain Anthony R. Whitaker

Captain Whitaker lost thirty-seven of his colleagues, officers in the Port Authority Police Department, including his old friend Officer Nathaniel "Nat" Webb, that morning, as well as many civilians who called him a friend. In the months that followed, people he never knew came up to him, some throwing their arms around him, thanking him for saving their lives. Like many who experienced that horrifying morning, today Tony has windows of time where he has no recall of the events that transpired. He personally considers it a blessing.

As horrifying as the events of that day were, and the days that followed, Captain Tony Whitaker maintained his sense of integrity and duty, and carried on in the finest tradition of the department. It wasn't long before he was promoted to assistant chief, and then to deputy chief/ chief of aviation, Port Authority of New York and New Jersey.

In February 2011, Tony retired.

Officer David Lim

Port Authority Police Officer David Lim, the six firefighters from Ladder Company 6, and Josephine Harris all survived the collapse from within the B-stairwell of the North Tower with little more than a few cuts and bruises, a broken bone, and one minor concussion.

As the air cleared, and after assessing their precarious predicament, they got on their radios and called in Maydays and 10-14s: officers requiring assistance. Officer Lim used his cell phone to call his wife, Diane, to inform her of his safe condition, and then passed it around for the firefighters and Josephine to call their families.

After nearly five hours of waiting, sitting on the unsteady stairs atop of what remained of the North Tower of the World Trade Center, Rescue Company 43 came to their rescue.

Officer David Lim kept his promise to return for his faithful friend and K-9 partner, Sirius. After four months, the remains of Sirius were recovered from the wreckage of Ground Zero. Workers immediately called David to the site, and with another officer, John Martin, Officer

David Lim carried out the remains of Sirius with full honors, complete with a prayer. All machinery stopped, an American flag was draped over the body bag, and all workers at the rescue and recovery site stood at attention and saluted—rendering upon Sirius honors equal to those given to recovered police officers and firefighters.

"I fulfilled my promise to him," David said. "I came back and took him home."

Helena Marietta

Helena outran the dark, billowing cloud that was determined to devour her. But her bare feet paid the price. Her more serious cuts were stitched and she was treated for numerous lacerations. It was late in the day when she finally arrived, both physically and mentally exhausted, at her little apartment in New Jersey.

As she watched the coverage on television, awestruck at what she was seeing, the realization of what she had survived began to take its toll. She had made many friends in her short eight months in the Twin Towers, and now it seemed that none of them had survived. Had it not been for the late night with her boyfriend, and her consequently sleeping through her alarm, she realized that she too would have been counted as one of the victims. She puzzled at the seeming haphazardness of timing, and briefly wondered if there wasn't more to life than met the eye.

After a couple months of introspection and much soul-searching, Helena got rid of her few possessions, packed her bags, kissed her boyfriend—who, in a way, had saved her life—good-bye, and took the bus back to the safety and security of her daddy's Montana horse ranch.

Nancy D. Seliga

Nancy and Bob Benacchio walked to the Holland Tunnel where they were driven in a Port Authority Police car to the Port Authority Technical Center in Jersey City. They immediately began networking, making lists of people they knew were safe, and those yet unaccounted for. Nancy was able to talk with her husband, Chuck, who had turned around at 8:48 a.m. as he was driving to a business trip in Boston. Working the phones at the Technical Center by day, and from her home at night, by Friday she was beyond exhausted.

Chuck took her to dinner that evening just to get her out of the house and to give her a break from it all. When they returned home there was a message from their son, Chris, on the answering machine, and Chuck returned the call.

"Nancy," Chuck said, "Chris wants to talk to you."

"I can't talk to him," she replied. Her nerves were shot. Between the emotions of the past eighty-five hours, all of her best friends being dead, and the lists of people still unaccounted for, Nancy couldn't stop crying.

"You really need to talk to him, Nancy," Chuck insisted.

"Hello," she said weakly, sobbing into the phone.

"God almighty!" Chris emphasized. "I'm finally getting to you before your first grandchild is born."

"What!?"

"We knew on the tenth and were going to tell everyone on the eleventh, but you had the audacity to let two towers fall down around you!"

Nancy was beside herself, sobbing, crying, sniffling . . .

"What are you crying for?" he asked forcefully.

"Because I'm so happy," she replied, both laughing and crying at the same time.

Nancy was one of a three-member team that contacted the wives, husbands, and families of the seventy-five deceased Port Authority of New York and New Jersey employees. She did yeoman's work, giving 100 percent of herself to the demands, discretion, and patience this responsibility required.

As the missing pieces were put back into place, Nancy was assigned to Newark Liberty International Airport and, after a few years of additional exceptional service, with mixed emotions reluctantly accepted the opportunity to retire.

Victor M. Guarnera

Vic Guarnera dragged himself toward the Stuyvesant High School principal's office. His right leg was throbbing and he was beginning to limp. Then he heard that the Pentagon had been attacked. Someone announced that he smelled gas in the school, so everyone was evacuated. Back on the street, Vic found a pay phone and tried telephoning his wife, Carmela, to tell her that he had survived. The call didn't connect. He was totally exhausted, but continued to hobble up West Street when he ran into two colleagues, Mike Hurley and Rich Pietruski.

"You look like hell!" they said to Vic. "Come on, let us help you." They took him to an open fire hydrant, removed his suit jacket, and shook out a pound of gritty dust while Vic stuck his head under the running water. He was surprised to discover that grit caked his face and filled his mouth, and that his hair was full of dirt and pieces of debris, as was the rest of his body. He was a mess. Mike, Rich, and Vic walked to the corner and ran into PAPD Captain Anthony Whitaker. Vic and Tony hugged a hug only those who have stared death in the face could appreciate. Then George Tabeek, Carla Bonacci, and Alan Reiss trickled in and joined them. A reunion was taking place and it was an emotional one.

A pedestrian came along, recognized what he was observing, and offered his cell phone to Vic. "Do you want to try and reach home?" he asked.

"Oh, thank you. What do I owe you?"

"Nothing. If you're successful, just go ahead and do it," he replied.

A female voice answered.

"Hello, Mel?" Vic asked, using his affectionate name for his wife, Carmela.

"Who is this?"

"Mel?"

"Who is this?" the female voice asked again.

"Goddamnit, who is *this!*" Vic blurted out. Between the traumatic events and the pressure of grit forced into his ears during the collapse, Vic's hearing was traumatized. "Is Carmela there?" he asked again with emphasis.

"Daddy! Daddy! Daddy!" his daughter, Dawn, screamed, and Carmela picked up the phone.

"Hun," Vic told her gently, "put away the black clothes. You're not a widow yet. I'm out, but I'm going to find out what we can do here before I let you know when I'm coming home."

"Okay. Thank you," she replied slowly, softly, relieved, almost not believing her good fortune.

"I love you, Mel."

Captain Whitaker called up a squad car and they all piled in. The Holland Tunnel was closed to all civilian traffic and they drove ninety-five miles per hour through it to Jersey City. They were dropped off at the Port

Authority Technical Center, Police Headquarters, where they were led to the showers and given clean clothes and bags to dispose of their caked, torn, and bloodstained clothing. Vic's leg was treated in the medical facility, and then they busied themselves putting together a command center. The phones began ringing and the numbers of the deceased and missing slowly began to come in. The televisions were broadcasting and, through his exhaustion, it began to dawn on Vic the magnitude of the disaster.

Vic finally got home to his family around 11:30 that evening. The wonderfully loving reunion with his wife, Mel, and his family would be forever etched in his memory.

In the weeks and months that followed, Vic worked the command center, and at the World Trade Center site with the rescue and recovery teams. On June 11, 2002, for his many acts of courage and selflessness on September 11, he was presented the Civilian Commendation Award for Bravery, Heroism, and Valor.

Vic retired from the Port Authority in October 2007 and is currently enjoying spending time with his family and grandchildren.

Tad Hanc

On his way home, heading uptown, bystanders, spectators—New Yorkers all—handed their cell phones to Tad Hanc. Someone even offered him a half-consumed bottle of Gatorade. He used a proffered cell phone to call his wife and family members to let them know he was okay. Walking north, he hoped to catch a bus or a subway, but nothing was running. When he flagged down a cab around Fourteenth Street, the cabby took one look at his sooty, bloodied condition, told him that he was not going uptown, and drove off. After a couple of hours walking uptown, he eventually caught a ride from a Good Samaritan. Tad arrived home at about 2:00 p.m. to the welcoming, open arms of his wife, Grazyna.

Tad showered, tossed all of his clothing into the trash bin, and with his wife had three fingers of scotch to help him calm down. Of all his friends and colleagues in the Twin Towers, Tad still thought he was one of the only few survivors. Sitting, watching television, he found it difficult to fully comprehend the images that repeated themselves over and over and over . . . the images of the towers collapsing. He still couldn't believe it. But he was home, safe, with Grazyna. His Mis'. His Little Bear.

Sarah Ronningen

Sarah watched television all day with Liz Kelly, Jackie Karpiloff, and her two adult children, Lisa and Joseph. Each scene—the impacts, the fireballs, the collapse, the cloud—became more and more surreal, and less and less encouraging with each showing. The ring of every phone call brought with it the hope of good news of Erik and Jackie's husband, Doug. Erik's safety was confirmed in the early afternoon by a phone call from friends who lived in midtown Manhattan, bringing immense relief to Sarah, and continued hope for the Karpiloffs.

The thought of living out the remainder of her days without her life's love and longtime companion had weighed heavily upon Sarah. It was perhaps, she considered, the most difficult day of her life, notwithstanding surgery for colon cancer seven years prior.

Sarah continued working for the Greenwich Association of Realtors until her second surgery for colon cancer in June of 2002, at which time she switched to part-time status. In June 2004, after her third surgery, she retired from the association, and cherished her remaining six months with her husband, Erik, at their home in Mamaroneck, New York.

Sarah passed away December 31, 2004.

Erik O. Ronningen

I stepped out of the deli sanctuary into the smoke-filled morning to head back to the World Trade Center. I wanted to contribute what efforts I could, but for the fourth time that morning, that quiet, little voice instructed *walk east*. And for the fourth time I obeyed. I turned, stepped right, and began walking toward the East River, and eventually discovered I was on the Bowery walking uptown.

Thousands of people were evacuating lower Manhattan, and the farther north I walked, the more of an anomaly I became. People began to offer me their cell phones to call home. News crews gave me impromptu interviews. Fifty people at a time would surround me, peppering me with questions. It was obvious where I had been; my hair was thickly matted gray, my trousers were rolled up to my knees, my blue pinstriped suit had a thick coating of gray matter, my brand-new wing-tip shoes looked like gray suede, and my black briefcase and black knee-length socks were all gray. I looked like the Pillsbury Doughboy.

Friends in midtown took me into their home. When Lee answered the door, she gave me a quick once-over and began laughing. It was contagious and I began laughing too, the tension dissipating. I showered—two or three times—dressed in loaner clothing, ate, and eventually made my way up to Grand Central Terminal once the Metro-North Railroad began running.

I had learned from Lee that my wife, Sarah, was at the home of Jackie Karpiloff, the wife of the director of security and life safety for the World Trade Center. I had barely gotten out of my car when all five foot, four inches, 120 pounds of my beautiful wife came running toward me, slamming into me and hugging me tightly.

Regional communications were a mess, but I discovered that the Internet was working and spent the next four days at home on my computer trying to determine who, and who had not, survived. On Saturday, I received a phone call asking if I'd man the emergency operations center at Journal Square in Jersey City. By the time all the lists were compiled, I could count over four dozen of my friends, associates, and acquaintances who had not survived the collapse of the Twin Towers.

Sarah, my wife of more than thirty-four years, was a rock of support, compassion, and understanding. To this day, I don't know how I would have made it through the following years—the survivor's guilt, the memory problems, and the odd assortment of physical and mental inconveniences—without the wonderful support of Sarah.

On September 11, 2001, I came within fourteen minutes of becoming a permanent employee with the Port Authority of New York and New Jersey. The two key people to make it happen, Executive Director Neil Leven and Doug Karpiloff, never made it out of the towers that morning.

As of this writing, I continue to work as a consultant at the Port Authority of New York and New Jersey in the Office of Emergency Management.

I fooled myself in the early months following 9/11, thinking that I *was* thinking clearly and acting calmly and rationally. I soon became aware that there were days when my thinking was labored. I had extreme difficulty retaining simple facts in my day-to-day business and private life. I would set off to tell someone something, and twenty minutes later return having no idea what I had set off to accomplish. I became disinterested in documenting details; I didn't know where to file papers and let material pile up on my desk, tossing it out after a few weeks because, looking at it, I didn't know what it was for. My head would fill up with dizziness, and there were times I thought I would have to lie on the floor to keep from falling. At frequent intervals, it felt like there was a giant beach towel stuffed between my brain, my eyes, ears, and mouth, so long was the time it took me to comprehend and respond to simple questions.

I was fully aware that this was not my pre-9/11 condition, and wondered how long I could continue to function before the folks I worked for—and with—found me out for the inept employee that I thought I was becoming. But then, I would consider that each of them had suffered through similar or worse experiences than I had that morning . . .

My sinuses ran continuously, everything in my body ached, a little irritating cough refused to go away, and I was urinating fifteen to twenty times daily. My associates affectionately gave me the moniker The Whiz Kid. And certain sounds and vibrations would set me off. As bad as all this sounds on paper, no one but Sarah and my friend and associate Vic Guarnera knew that I was having this internal struggle.

But I was not alone. People were breaking out in boils, coughing up black mucus, and had sores that would not heal, incessant itching, respiratory difficulties, and other conditions. The doctors had to open a whole new chapter on the physical problems people began showing up with that were directly related to 9/11.

One of the little pleasures I continue to have when I am at the World Trade Center site is to schedule enough time to walk the lines of tourists. I enjoy approaching the young ones, kids of ten or twelve, and asking them if they have any questions. In no time at all, I'll have spent an hour and a half fielding questions from people from all over the world. I enjoy giving them a little extra something to take home with them from their visit to New York City, and the effort they made to find their way downtown to visit the World Trade Center.

To say that the events of 9/11 were an amazing and extraordinary experience would be an understatement. I lost many friends and colleagues in that hour and forty-two minutes. And I know the emptiness of loss. However, opportunities have presented themselves to me that otherwise would not have. I have spoken to dozens and dozens of people about their thoughts on what happens after death. I have had many conversations about not taking for granted our relationships with spouses, families, and friends, for our circumstances can change in an instant. And our regrets— at realizing our selfishness and failure to cooperate with the most important people in our lives—can last a lifetime.

This experience has provided the opportunity to gain strength, to reevaluate previous efforts, to assist others to be strong, and to learn not to repeat mistakes.

Had I known what was in store for me that day, I would not have awakened to my 5:30 a.m. alarm. But having experienced that incredible morning, and having survived the collapses, the chaos, and all that followed—I don't know how to express this, but I would have been extremely displeased to have missed any aspect of that remarkable morning, and the days, months, and years that followed.

Thank you for listening . . .

ACKNOWLEDGMENTS

Certainly, to all who so generously gave of their time to relate their harrowing experiences from that morning, I am most grateful. These conversations have brought a greater depth of understanding to the magnitude of the events, and have shown me how personal are our individual trials, tribulations, and triumphs of 9/11.

I extend my gratitude to my old friend, Liz Stone who agreed to proof the first rough drafts and offered many valuable suggestions that I wisely accepted, as well as to my sister, Kaia Rayburn for her unselfish transcription services, without which this recollection of history would not have been possible.

Terry Morrell of Ambassador Medical Services, Inc., the Operations Manager for my Personnel Assurance Program, has championed this book and my poor efforts since we met in 2009, for which I am deeply appreciative.

Special thanks go to my agent and old-time friend of forty-eight years, Greg Oviatt, who, on friendship alone took on this project, and to my copy editor, Meredith Hale, whose patient tenacity corrected my many sophomoric errors in grammar, spelling, composition, syntax, and whatever all else goes into "cleaning copy." To my publisher, John Weber of Welcome Rain, I owe much appreciation for his faith in this work so many years afterward; an event that seems like yesterday.

My old colleague and friend Jim Usher deserves especial merit in that not only is his morning represented within these pages, he graciously allowed me the privilege of using his private and very personal photograph as the cover, reflecting the harrowing experiences taking place within the towers. And to Kevin Ullrich, art director extraordinaire who performed the magic to transform Jim's dramatic photograph from old digital technology to reflect the pain of emotion that morning brought and the ever-present tenacity that is the American Spirit.

I could not have begun this book without the loving encouragement of my wife, Sarah, nor completed it without my family, and the many friends and colleagues who encouraged me to bring to a successful conclusion this minute piece of history in a world-changing event.

Thank you all . . .

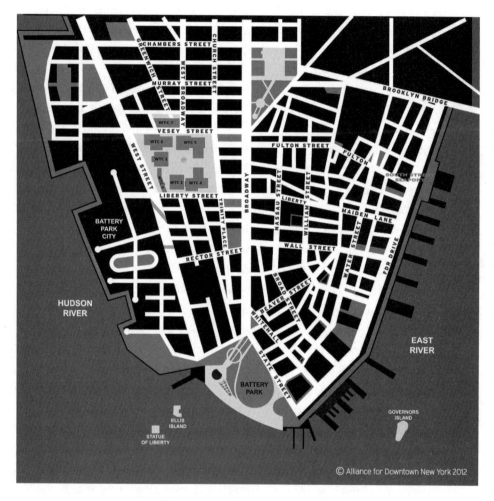

Map of Lower Manhattan, circa 9/11/2001

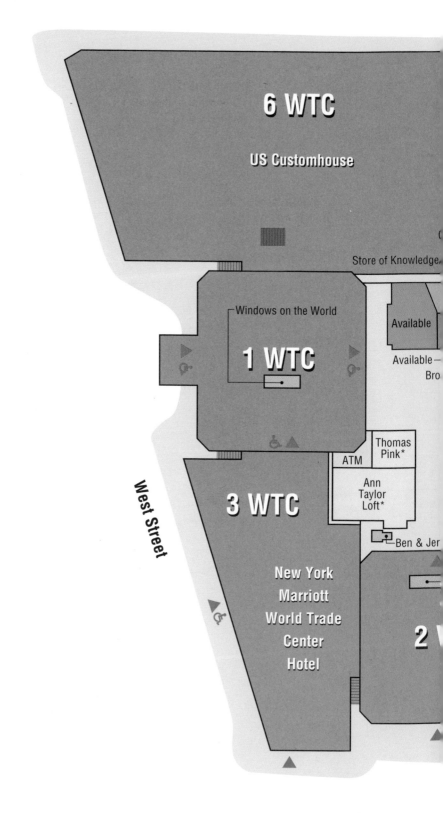

6 WTC

US Customhouse

Store of Knowledge

Windows on the World

1 WTC

Available

Available—
Bro

Thomas
Pink*

ATM

Ann
Taylor
Loft*

Ben & Jer

3 WTC

New York
Marriott
World Trade
Center
Hotel

2 W

West Street